Documentation in Insurance

By Kavita Sinha

Hello and I welcome you to this book. The objective of this book is to enable you as a student or as an employee, to understand the concepts relevant to software creation for automation.

Automation of processes was not pre – dominant some time back. In today's world, it exists across all industries. There may be many times when responsibilities in this discipline have to be taken on at work. Hence, learning agility is an important skill set needed nowadays when there is a rapid shift in technology.

What you learn from this book helps you to readjust your skill sets for the future and adds value to your position. This book helps you to get familiar with the concepts that are pivotal to the world of technology in industry.

The book focusses on EDP concepts and programming right from the beginning. The book embarks you on a journey through imperative concepts in business processes, setting requirements for the business processes and business system as it is developed in todays' technological driven world.

The book is a must read for intermediate students, working professionals and anyone who is interested in knowing about how we have reached so far in the implementation of technology. Though this book focuses on important developments in modern technology for the insurance industry, the same may be relevant for any industry.

This book has been designed with the academic and professional background that I have in the field. The source of my research is mainly the book titled 'Information Technology' from Insurance Institute of India. Following academic pursuits and updates by experts in the field and participating in group discussions on the topics are my references. The book is easy to read and helpful to get you started in the discipline.

Kavita Sinha

FIII, PGDM (Fin and CRM)

Activities and automation

In an organization, things that a person or a group of persons do, to meet business objectives, are known as activities. In business, activities denote monetary and non – monetary transactions which are done to meet business objectives. For example, a customer completes a proposal form (activity) and pays the premium (activity) to purchase an insurance policy (objective).

In the business world, activities are initiated by an event. An event occurs when activities are done or are to be done. For example: A refund is enumerated and made, daily/weekly/monthly information reports are printed, a policy is underwritten and receipt printed. Events are an outcome of mutual objectives of individuals and are completed when the goal is achieved.

Inconsistencies in business transactions also constitute as events. For example, some clients pay premium through bank notes or through demand draft, which are not accepted by the insurer. Such constraints are identified and revised processes are considered for the event to take place. Undoubtedly, events are caused by mutual objectives of persons and are bounded by organizational rules which keep changing and updating over the passage of time.

The amount of information needed could however become large and cumbersome. Events become difficult to complete manually. For example: Finding the insurance policy docket when we have just the name of the insured, getting the list of policies and claims over a period of the last five years. Moreover, speed and efficiency become paramount. This has led to the need for automation of activities. In fact, logical programming and automation has stepped in almost all spheres of individual and business activities.

PROGRAMMING AND DATA MANAGEMENT

Programs are sets of instructions that form the software of the computer's system. Programs can be understood by the computer. These sets of instructions are usually written in **high level languages**, are converted into low level/machine language/codes by translators, interpreters and compilers

Instructions that build programs can be classified into four groups: Arithmetic operations, compare and test operations, jump/branch instructions, input/output instructions.

Programs work with data that are stored in files. The data stored in the computer are arranged by the hierarchy of data representation. Data representation in files is as follows:

BIT: This forms the communication interface with the machine which gives the 'on' and 'off' signals. The BIT is the single binary digit having a value of o or 1.

Byte: These are constituted by a group of 8 bits that initiate a specific sequence of signals. This character code of ASCII is formed by a group of 7 or 8 bits.

Fields: These are a group of Bytes. They represent the basic unit of input. There could be any number of bytes that makes a field. They give information about one item at a time. Examples of fields include name, age, and document number.

Record: A number of fields that are related in some way to form a detail and make a record. There could be any number of fields to make a record. For example the details of the proposal form include name, age, cover required, premium.

File: A group of related records form a file. The records forming a file may vary in length. Examples of records include the following: (1) the policy file has the list of all policy holders (2) the personnel file has the list of all employees (3) the claims reported file has the list of all the claims reported.

EDP and data management

Electronic data processing denotes the conversion of raw data into the required output or information. What is data? Data consists of records in the form of figures, words, charts or symbols. Some examples of input data are policy, cash receipts and claims vouchers. These are also called as primary sources of data.

Electronic data processing is done by the Data Base Management System. The DBMS connects interrelated fields in data by using the Structured Query Language (SQL). DBMS allows access to data and allows modification of the database. The DBMS enables data to be stored and arranged according to a particular order. The DBMS also allows a number of users to access the database.

In the popular form of representation the DBMS stores and arranges the data hierarchically in a prescribed order. In a more complex form of representation, data is represented in relation with each other (Networked /relationally). In this data model, data is stored and processed in the form of tables which are also called as relations.

EDP system in the insurance industry

The data inputs for software are primarily 'fields' and 'records'. These are analyzed and processed within the **Data Based Management System**. The output is known as 'processed data' or 'information' for decision making. Specified data is processed in 'modules'. A 'module' represents a department. In certain cases modules are interconnected. The output in one module becomes an input in another module. For example, the receipts register which is the output in the accounts module becomes the input for the claims module where the receipts particulars are verified.

EDP of the Insurance Policy Module

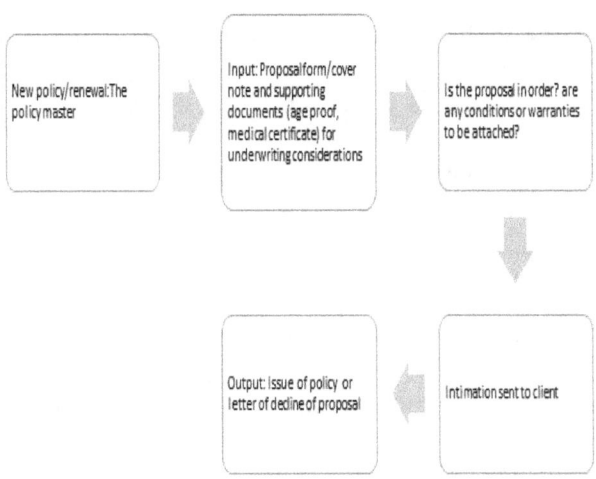

EDP of the Insurance Claims Module

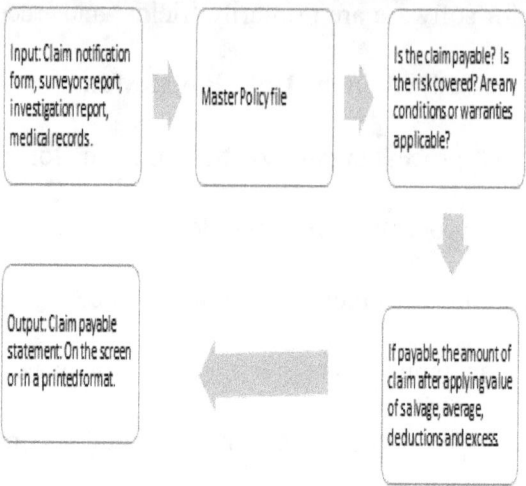

Explanation: The input data are records that are stored in the master file. For example: during an underwriting event, a proposal form received from a customer is the input, during a claim event a claim intimation form received from a claimant is the input. Other documents received such as surveyor's report number, investigation report number and medical bills received are inputs.

The master file data is referred to by the DBMS and the input data is correlated and analyzed with existing records. From confirming existing policy details (for renewals) and the validity status of the policy (for the claims), numerous required reports are analysed from the master file data by the DBMS. Data assimilated and analyzed and made into meaningful information by DBMS, is used to arrive at and implement decisions. For example: whether a proposal form can be accepted and underwritten, whether a claim has been verified and is payable, whether deductions are applicable and other terms and conditions. The decision is made in the form of a screen display or a printed form.

Information management enabled by DBMS enables the organization to make timely decisions. Information requirements differ by the persons using them and the purpose of usage. For example, different sets of information are required by the chairman, the branch manager and the operating manager and employees. This type of specific information is obtained by establishing some **data relationships** within the DBMS. Besides, **predictive analysis** between inputs and outputs and **software solutions for business processes** is formulated by data relationships. Undoubtedly, EDP processes enabled by DBMS are indispensable as they provide a means for getting the required information systematically that is relevant and logical.

SOME RELEVANT SKILLS: Big Data, Hadoop, Analytics

Exercises

Outline the EDP parameters of your organization.

Hint: Identify and make of list activities, event objectives of the organization. Then identify and list the inputs and outputs which are the outcome of each of the events.

Programs become important because they enable processes. Programs refer to instructions given and understood by the computer. They are maintained in the storage area within the Central Processing Unit of a computer. Programming elements are assigned codes which control how the **data is managed and utilized**. The two prime concepts in computer programming are:

Algorithm: This is a simple instructional language that forms the protocol and enables operations to be performed in sequential order.

Flow Chart: Flow charts trace out logical functions. They are diagrammatic representations of the logic of computer programs. The logical representation gives a step to step path for constructing processes. At the outset, we need to become familiar with the fundamental functions of flow charts. Some popular flow chart functions are:

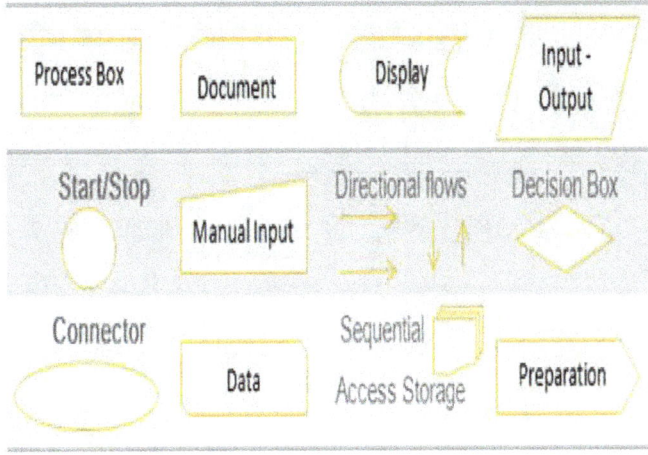

A program 'starts', 'reads', 'computes', 'decides', 'displays', 'prepares' and 'stops' after all the inputs have been 'read'. The sequence is set by the protocol of the algorithms.

The illustration given here is a flow chart for a program for a tax module. This illustration helps us understand the fundamental functions of a flow chart and how they are used to make programs.

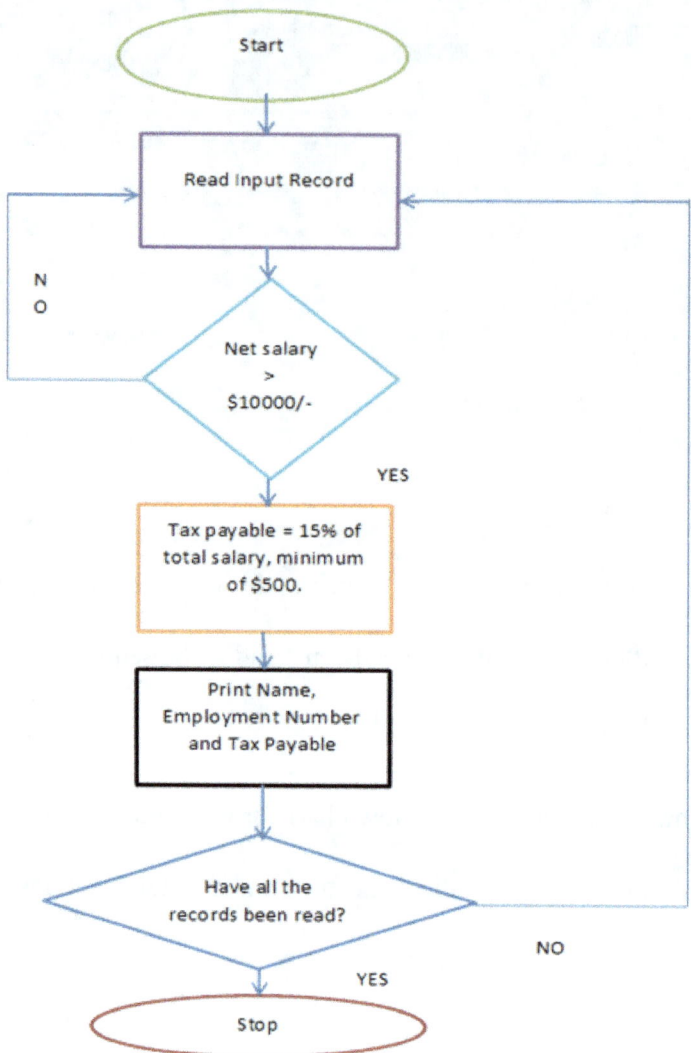

On the completion of this program flow chart, the language and coding preferences are chosen. And so, the flow charts' sequences are written and coded in the preferred language and coding combination.

Programming Methods: While the two most important concepts of programming are algorithms and flowcharts, the most important methods of programming are procedural, object –oriented – programming and event driven programming.

Procedural Programming: This is the *fundamental method* of programming. They include procedural languages like BASIC, C, PASCAL and ASSEMBLY. Procedural programs are designed by coding or by assigning a 'procedure', a 'routine', 'subroutine' and a 'function' to specific data. This formats data. The programming 'element' which is constituted by the 'formatting' of specific data (by assigning program codes) is called as a 'named group of statements'. These are done to make the programs work according to the specifications of the user and create the 'software'.

Object –Oriented Programming: Object - oriented programming is done in addition to procedural programming. Object oriented programming permits programmers to work on the 'problem' *as they are to be solved.* Hence, OOP is constituted by both procedures and objects. For this, the object oriented language package has a collection of pre –defined **'base objects'** or **'classes'** which are combinations of variables, functions and data structures. In other words, the objects are **'data – sets'** and are assigned codes. The data sets are used as building blocks to create additional required classes. These are the 'solution sets' and can be used within corporate networks and the internet. Object oriented programming languages include C++, C#, Python, PHP, Java, Pearl and Ruby.

Event Driven Programming: Event driven programming *enables user interactivity.* A program cannot understand on its own that it has to function. When using a computer, almost all programs that are to be utilized, has the interaction of the user.

So far we have learnt about procedural and object – oriented programming which enables the computer to work according to the instructions. However, we need a functionality that enables the user to preform various tasks on the computer screen as well, For example, entering data on a website and working with a specific location on the screen. To enable these functionalities, a programmer needs a language that enables interaction between the computer and the user. What works well here is event driven programming.

Event driven programs is made by 'language implementations'. This type of programming has the ability to detect all possible events that can occur during the interaction between the user and the computer. The detection is made possible by the computers language compilers (or the operating system's API) and is not done manually one by one by the programmer. The BASIC language by itself is not event driven programming. The Windows API is an event driven program. Here is where you can develop applications. Windows API is focused mainly on the programing language C: They provide capabilities to (Microsoft Visual Basic's) MS-DOS. The additional functionalities provided by Windows API are graphic device interface, a user interface and also networking capabilities of the operating system.

Event driven programming enables a user to enter data by a keyboard or a mouse, to work with any function of the keys on the keyboard and work with the click of the mouse at a specific location on the screen.

Program Design and the IT department

So far we have learnt that programs are designed to be run on an operating environment along with a database. Programs for **constructing business processes** are designed by giving proper specifications. These specifications are created on the **'workspace'** which the team is working with.

These specifications include:

The program design and logic: The program design and logic defines what the program is expected to do and what the outcomes and their impacts should be. The logic is represented in the form of flow diagrams as we have learned earlier. They form the basis of programming.

The input and output format: Input and output formats are specified and designed to be used with the database. The formats determine the number of specifications like records per line and speed and efficiency in utilization of screen space.

The file layout: The file layout specifies how data is viewed by the user. Here the fonts, colors and arrangement of information are done. The layout should enable reading and writing and arranging the data structure.

The run – chart: The run - chart is maintained to identify past and current trends in the business process. The run - chart indicates whether variables have changed, will change or remain stable over time.

The test scheduling of the programs: This ongoing process validates each and every stage of development of the project. Test scheduling establishes the stage of the project which is under progress, whether it has been completed and is ready for final testing.

The objectives

Business process applications are enabled processes to automate the business processes. Hence, resources are deployed for setting up and maintaining business process applications. In such a situation, the **organizations' IT department** becomes important.

The Role

The role of IT department includes providing the latest hardware and software resources so as to make the company competitive. These resources should provide a *high payback method* of reaching the goals of the stakeholders. The business automation solution should provide for **effectivity in automation** by enabling improved decision making and implementation. Automation should result in lowering of costs, earning higher revenues and *increasing profit abilities.*

The organization is restructured to viably provide for *local and global markets.* The organization should also efficiently and effectively achieve compliance with the *state government regulatory and corporate governance requirements.* Another important role of the IT department is to encourage the business environment to imbibe innovations.

The skill sets

In the modern scenario, the existing processes and applications may not be able to make cutting edge business activities. The existing processes may need to be upgraded and made more comprehensive.

Basic process models are made by identifying the stakeholders, the start events, tasks, finding solutions and implementing the solutions. Alternatively, the management may consider buying or building a packaged application for the business which can help in streamlining activities and processes. In any event some skills are required.

1) Analytical thinking and problem solving:

The analyst has to identify the constraints and inadequacies of the existing business processes. Then the analyst should evaluate the requirements for relevant processes by interviewing stakeholders. The analyst also has the following functions:

- Establishing the cost – benefit of the project,

- Mapping the do's and dont's of what is to be done

- Formulating revised and/or new business processes

- Formulating the needs of the target audience and transmitting information via e –mail, presentation or a website

2) Technical and domain knowledge:

The analyst has the following roles to perform:

- Understand what the problem is within the domain requirements.

- Analyze the constraints and rebuilding capacity of the existing domain processes.

- How the problem could be solved by domain based processes?

- What resources are required towards arriving at the solution?

- Do all these activities fall within the company's strategy/policy?

- Will they be able to meet with cost and quality constraints?

- *Programming Languages and Implementation:* Examples: Java, Python, C++ and Microsoft Visual Basic.

- Identify processes for strategic changes, up gradations and for continuing processes.

Training

Business Process Analysis deals with identifying, analyzing and documenting the existing processes. The inputs, outputs, the step by step processes and roles of the 'actors' (the ones who do the tasks) are considered in the existing state. An analysis is made of the current process to find out ways to make the process more efficient. A system that has to be upgraded requires this type of 'Current State Analysis' to be made for all the processes. Then, the impact of the proposed changes in processes is studied.

For all this to become real, the training programs for the IT team are designed. The objective of the training is to empower the trainees with indispensable capabilities. The trainees should learn to impart details about the project and their proposed solutions to the stakeholders. They could even produce a prototype (a simulation of the final product) to the stakeholders.

They should acquire competency in business process mapping and designing standard processes which defines what the business is set up to do. All this means that the team should join on board the workspace and learn to work and navigate within the workspace. For example, working with workspaces like 'waterfall; 'agile' on software platforms like 'jira' or 'open stack' for enabling a cloud platform. This also means determining the parameters that make the business successful and identifying when and how improvements can be made for business efficiency.

The project manager

The project manager should be able to determine and make accountable, the persons who do the tasks and the persons who are responsible for its completion. At the same time, standards should be set for work and output performance.

Organizational readiness

This process of automation of business activities involves strategic planning by the owners and management team. This is meant to enable greater efficiency and productivity. This however necessitates the deployment of additional resources. Besides, the entity needs to have some resilience for such changes to take place. It needs to be determined whether or not the organization has the capacity to sustain changes.

Take the case of an individual student planning on a new activity like golf. Does the individual have enough time and resources and the flair? Does their potential and interest help them become a professional golf player?

Take the case of a business entity planning a new product line. Given the intention the following factors have to be considered:

- Can the entity be seen as having sustainable capacity for these changes?

- Is a new activity line feasible in terms of cost and time?

- How are the activities organized at present?

- Is there individual and collective skill and motivation among employees and is there executive commitment of the owner and management?

New processes and activities may induce shock and imbalances. The illustration below gives us the parameters that can be used to assess the organizational readiness and capacity to sustain such shocks and imbalances.

Type of organization - Functional, Matrix, Project type	Number of skilled and unskilled workers	Level of research and knowledge
Conventional or modern level of technology	Training capabilities are little or advanced	Resource mobilizationa and utilization capacities.
Employee motivation present or not present.	Collaborative skills present or not present	Stratergy. vision, mission, social, political environment

The inherent analyst

In daily life, there are many ways in which an individual may have performed the work of an analyst. An artist, for example, will know how much of work there is in each and every painting that has to be completed, and the difficulty level. The artist may set some target mark to be achieved, allot time and space to study and probably make a time table to practice the skill beforehand. The artist will also realize that just sitting down to paint is not all, but the quality of painting depends on their aptitude at that point in time. These already seem to be a lot of parameters to consider and work upon.

Similarly, a manager, leader or employee may have already performed the work of an analyst while working with business activities and plans. The manager may have assigned a specific time span for the team to work upon a task. Activities are assigned to the team members to achieve objectives and targets. The manager assimilates and analyzes data to improve the processes by which the work is done, and suggests new products and processes. All this involves analytical thinking, working with and implementing business plans and upgrading processes. These are all part and parcel of the work of an analyst.

Exercises

Identify business processes. Draw a simple flow chart that can make the program.

Hint: Refer to the example on taxation given earlier in the chapter.

Assess organizational readiness in your entity.

The Stakeholders

The owners of the business work towards profitability as their main goal. Moreover, the governments expect compliance with rules and regulations, creditors require timely repayment of loans and the customers seek good service and good products at a reasonable rate. So we can infer from here, that **many parties are interlinked** with the activities and performance of the organization. These parties are called **stakeholders**. There are a number of stakeholders in a business system and they can be classified as internal stakeholders and external stakeholders.

Internal Stakeholders	*External Stakeholders*
Owners	The Shareholders
Employees and Staff	Suppliers
The Management	Customers
Partners	Creditors and Financiers
Employees Family	Government, Environment

Stakeholders include the owners, employees, customers, suppliers, government and the environment and influence the activities of the organization in some way or the other. In turn, stakeholders are influenced by the activities of the organization and are interested to know whether the business should be perceived as efficient, effective and earns planned profits. Therefore, the interests of the stakeholders are primary and are kept as the most important criteria to uphold sustainability.

Collaboration

The designated managers of the users' team and the IT team communicate with each other and collect relevant information and data. They do this to analyze the factors that are necessary to establish the **new or revised processes** and to arrive at time and cost **agreements**. As time and cost are involved, there is a need for 'collaboration' between the owners, the IT team and any other stakeholders who are concerned with the timing and costing of the project.

Characteristics

Stakeholders are disparate and not all the stakeholders are the same or equal. Some are more important than others. The capacities and intention of these stakeholders should be **judged individually**. Some stakeholders prefer not to interrelate with one another. Here, some sort of goodwill has to be established. Some stakeholders are influential and may have plenty of interest. A good strategy here would be to keep these stakeholders well informed and up to date about the initiative. Some stakeholders may be yet unaware that there has been an initiative; others may be neutral to the initiative. Some stakeholders may not offer cooperation and support while others may participate and become part of the team. This assessment should not be a onetime process, but a continuous one throughout the term of the project.

Work can and will be done as and when there are resources and healthy relationships are maintained. Therefore, the **interpersonal relationships, preferences and characteristics** of the stakeholders are important considerations. It is important that the stakeholders participate and their inputs noted. An assessment is made about how the stakeholders influence activities. Some may be approachable while others may not be approachable. Some stakeholders are influential while others are non-influential:

Approachable and influential stakeholders: The maintenance of good relationships is required.	*Approachable but non influential stakeholders*: A continued collaboration will be an adequate approach for them.

Influential stakeholders but not approachable: Reaching out to them and initiating collaboration is a good strategy to follow.	Non-influential stakeholders and not approachable: They do not need to have much importance attached to them.

RESOURCES

The project team: The project team advises the management about Business Processes. They integrate the activities of both the business and IT team. They are responsible for integrating the latest hardware and software technology to maintain the competitive edge of the company. The project team is responsible for deploying the new or revised BPM processes. They use existing infrastructure and additional specified software and resources.

Project leader/ Manager: A senior executive is overall in charge of the software development project. The project manager plans and controls the movements of the two way flow of data (the input data and the output data) that fall within the scope of the project. For example, in an insurance company, the input data consists of proposals and claim notification details, accounting and investment details. The output data are in the layout of policy and claim documents and layout of accounting reports and so on.

The project manager plans the activity schedule, assigns tasks to the IT team, conducts periodical reviews, coordinates the functions of the team activities and keeps tab on KPI's.

Domain experts*:* Domain experts provide insight about the processes and events of the entity. They also provide some ideas and suggestions to improve the processes. Their presentations are made for an industry wise study and rundown on the requirements for the company.

Systems designers and analyst: The systems designers and analysts develop computer programs and procedures for the organization, to meet the business and informational requirements. They study the existing procedures, define problems, design the proposed business system, gain acceptance of the stakeholders, prepare required systems flow charts, implement and monitor and maintain the new design. As traditional roles see a contraction, the system analyst may need skills in cloud computing and big data analytics too.

Programmers and developers: Their role is to create computer programs according to the system application requirements. Developing and maintaining the program are done by document filing, coding, interrelating, integration, testing and debugging of data.

Network administrators: Network administrators are the system administrators or operations manager. They have the crucial role of managing the networks. They oversee the live mode of the system set up and the security of data. They oversee the source data of various departments like the underwriting, claims and accounts department. They create user rights and security of passwords of supervisor and users, loading new software and suggest changes and improvements. They oversee training for the operators and users. Miscellaneous functions include purchase of computer media including ink jets for printers, stationary and miscellaneous media, coordinating with the IT system designers and back up of the system software.

Operations' users: These parties use the computer for day to day activities. Depending on the job assigned to them, they perform underwriting, claims, accounts and communication by email all facilitated by computers. They are required to keep a back –up of data and report any problems faced if at all.

Software requirements:

Programmed software platforms include (Java platform, Microsoft XNA, Silverlight, Open web platform, .NET framework, Oracle database, Windows runtime and so on) and are specifically selected to work with. The **programs** are developed and maintained within the operating system. A **backend database** is used, which is made of tables to help retrieve information and store data. A **hypertext processor** and an **HTTPS server** are used, that can administer the backend database over the world wide internet.

Users: There are three sets of users

Admn and staff: The admin is the top level user of the system. The admin has access to the database and all the customer and agent records. They have the right to provide and oversee the creation of customer and agent IDs. The employees can create new policy and claims records. They work with the system in underwriting, claims and accounting and management services.

Agents: Agents can view details of each customer and update the status of the policy as 'pending' or 'running' or 'scrapped'. They have access to the premium and renewal collection information. They will be able to send intimation to customers according to the date of renewal. They can check the claims made by the customers.

Customers: Customers submit proposals for approval. They check details about their policy. They view information about the policy agent if the business was brought through an agent. The customer fills in the details of claims incurred along with the estimated claim amount.

Exercises

Your business needs to be automated. What are the issues that come up to solve this situation?

Hint: Estimate the resources and technology required. Estimate the time and cost of the proposed activities. Establish the concerns of all the persons who are involved and affected by the proposed solution.

THE REQUIREMENTS

About Elicitation

Elicitation begins with addressing the problem statement after which relevant data and information are gathered from all the concerned stakeholders. The 'as is' processes are analyzed. The 'to be' processes which are meant to resolve the problem statement, are to be worked out. These are the main considerations for the 'requirements documents'. The requirements documents are designed for setting up solutions within the budgeted costs. Hence, the documents help to identify and select the processes from the perspective of both the organization and the stakeholders. This is the also first stage of the life cycle of systems designing. Whilst defining requirements, many business 'events', 'scenarios' and 'stories' are analyzed. Hence, there may be a chance that all the efforts seem irrelevant at some point in time as they not make complete sense.

About Requirements gathering:

Requirements data are gathered through the process of elicitation.

The data collected are relevant to the needs of the proposed solution and must be testable.

All requirements building parameters may not be of equal importance. They are prioritized according to the standards and the assignments that the organization has to work upon.

The requirements are verified to make sure that they have been understood clearly.

Requirements are validated by making sure that they are explicitly agreed upon by all the stakeholders.

The initial findings are the feasibility study which gives the following information:

1) A diagrammatic representation of the current system.

2) The obstacles and constraints of the current system.

3) A logical representation of the proposed automated system.

4) Alternatives to the new model.

5) The advantages and a good estimate of the cost and time.

6) The requirements specification documents.

Requirements Specifications Documents

The requirements specification documents are designed by bifurcating applicable parameters as functional and non-functional. Hence, 'functional' and 'non-functional' diagrams are defined, marked and employed to set up solutions.

Functional requirements

The functional requirements document is the primary document for the system requirement specification. We start with the organization status quo and the current needs of the organization. The work and processes are identified and defined within various departments and groups. Work performed is traced by activity paths within and between departments. Hence, the FRS document marks - out the work and activity path. Then the question about how to improve business operations and customer relationships are addressed.

The four parts of the functional and domain requirements documents *which are all within the project platform or made independently as chosen and required.* They are: (1) the systems overview, (2) the functional specifications, (3) the user manual and (4) the program specifications.

Document 1: The system overview:

Initially, the current systems' layout, objectives and advantages are compared with the proposed system with the help of an organization chart. The proposed automated set up is laid out by data flow diagrams (DFD).

The detailed document is usually written in an easily understood mark-up language.

Illustration: Functional requirements of an insurance system

The website shall have a simple and minimalist homepage having only 8 functionalities.

To create an interactive and user friendly interface with no clutter.

Searching for insurance products on the website.

Customers access to filling proposals and filing claims online.

Easy navigation menu.

Enabling an online payment mode.

Agent's login, employee login and customer's login on the website interface.

Some administrative functions on the website.

Automation to be application rich and accessible on any device.

Pages to be easy and self-descriptive.

Users to have access to data base and also a subset of the database.

Each policy to be allocated a unique policy number, each claim to be allotted a unique claim number.

The user having access to the permanent storage area.

Underwriting: Proposal form, Cover Note, Cash Premium, Check Premium Payment, Online Premium Payment (Credit card/ debit card/net banking/wireless), Scrutiny of proposal, Acceptance of proposal, issuing of policy, renewal notice, endorsements and alterations of policy)

Claims: Intimation, Verification of policy details, issue of claim note, appointment of surveyors/investigators, documents submitted by insured, surveyors/investigators report, verification of documents, final claims assessment, issue of discharge voucher, claim payment made by check or online, collection of receipt from customer)

Accounts Department: Preparation of daily cash register, balance sheet, revenue account, profit and loss account, cash inflow and outgo account.

Management Services Department: Payroll, agency system, underwriting, claims and expenses report on a weekly, monthly, half yearly or yearly basis. Audit functions, regulation and corporate governance.

-------------*End of illustration*-------------

Document 2: Functional Specifications:

The functional specifications document follows the system overview and has the following information:

A flow diagram: A precise system flow diagram and system structure chart as worked out in the systems overview

The query list: The query list and the information requirements table (IRT). (Examples of IRT have been given later in this chapter.)

The code structure: This is done to enable the functionalities that make the software.

The input document format: The input documents include the interface for proposals, claims notifications and so on.

The output layouts: The output layouts include the interface for policy, claims and accounting reports and so on.

The file and records layout: These are the interface that provide information about all the documents.

System controls and validation techniques: These techniques are selected beforehand and implemented periodically throughout the term of the project.

The system standards: These are specified by the user and incorporated in the document.

Document 3: User Manual: The user manual gives the following information:

- The start-up procedures.

- The menu tree and the sequence of operations.

- Error messages giving explanations.

- Back – up procedures.

- Recovery procedures.

Document 4: Program Specifications

This document gives the program file table and call table.

Program 1	Name	Functions
Program 2	Name	Functions
Program3	Name	Functions

Document 5: The system requirement specifications (SRS):

The SRS is defined by the functional requirements specification document. The main function of SRS is to enable the working of the system according to the rules and regulations of the organization. It provides a description about what the functioning system should be capable of doing, defines the scope and organizes the boundaries of the decision making functions.

For this purpose, large functions (eg: underwriting, claims, accounting) are decomposed into smaller functions (according to IRT). It may be written in formal language as specified or a PDL (page description language). PDL is an important tool for software designing for systems designers and programmers.

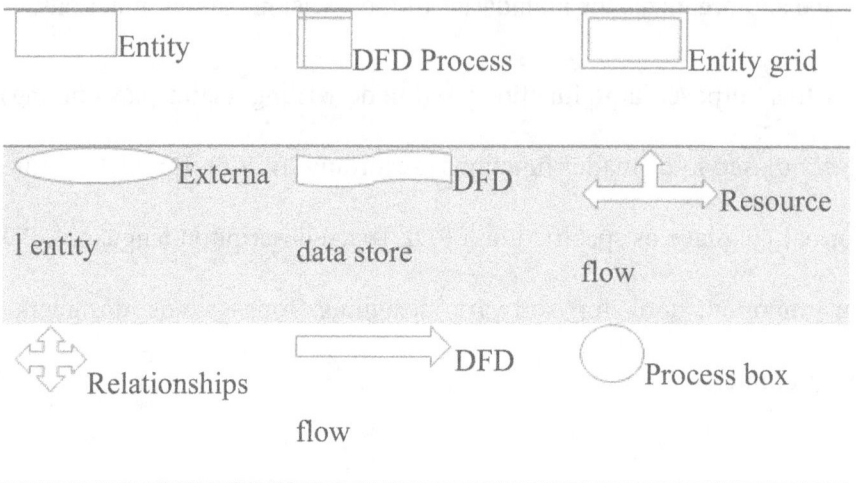

IRT for Motor Policy

COVERAGES		
Coverage A –	Liability:	Premium
Bodily Injury Claims	$2,00,000 each person	$100.00
	$4,00,000 each accident	
Property Damage Claims	$1,00,000 each accident	$50.00
Coverage B – Medical Payments	$15000 each person	$25.00
Coverage C –	Uninsured Motorists:	
Bodily Injury	$ 2,00,000 each person	$25.00
	$ 4,00,000 each accident	
	TOTAL	$200.00

COVERAGES	PERILS	INSURED	EXCLUSIONS
and	CONDITIONS		

Coverage A: Dwelling : Direct Physical Loss Damage

Coverage B: Other Structures

Coverage C: Personal Property

Coverage D: Loss of Use

Other Additional Coverages

1) List of Perils Excluded

2) Principal of Insurable Interest

3) Principal of Indemnity

4) Other principals, conditions and warranties

Non-functional requirements

Non – functional requirements are the building blocks of the software design. Non-functional requirements are planned for a conceptual model known as the 'system architecture' which is formally enabled by the 'architecture description languages ('ADL's). Non-functional requirements determine specific software elements and resolve constraints within the system design. On the whole, they refer to the overall system performance and not particularly to a specific function. The attributes of non – functional system requirements include the following:

Quality

Speed

Reliability

User friendliness

Capacity

Strength

Performance indexes like throughput response time, response usage, effect of overload conditions

Reliability standards like maximum down time, maximum known bugs, maximum failure rate and maximum down time

Testability and Availability

Security Failure Management

Configuration and Compliance

Efficiency

Effectiveness

Learnability

Training material

Online help

Non-functional decomposition is primary in software development. They help to remodel and make a prototype of a system. The objective is to recreate the system keeping in mind the needs of the stakeholders. Non – functional decomposition help to resolve conflicts brought about requirements and constraints, including inadequate time, level of complexity, capacity and standards of the system

Touchstones in Requirements Gathering:

***Frameworks*:** Frameworks are used to develop these documents for complex products that meet the requirements of the stakeholders. The frameworks used include 'Waterfall' and 'Agile'. 'Waterfall' is a project methodology involving analysis, designing, implementation, testing and evaluation of requirements. The methodology called 'Agile' has the additional feature of feedback after each stage of requirements gathering. The documentation in these frameworks includes Business Requirement Documents, Software Requirements Specification and Functional Specification Document. The team/characters are constituted by the owner, product owner, scrum master, scrum team, BA and QA lead. The Requirement Documents are built on concepts including Epic Stories, Backlog and User Stories.

Given below are the terminologies that are used in software methodologies.

***Detailing business needs*:** Business needs > Epics > User Requirements > User Stories > Use Cases > Product backlog items.

***Epic*:** These are high level requirements are what the user wants from the software. They are designed to be prepared in bits and pieces. Eg: I want: a policy module, a claims module and an accounts module. All these requirements become part of an Epic.

User requirements: Here, the end users state the requirements in narrative terms. For example; "I need an interactive customer platform for underwriting policies and intimating claims with an easy to use payment portal". User description should be documented in natural language, tables and diagram so that it can be easily understood by all the other stakeholders.

User stories: User stories include a short description of the problem or need, and are written from the angle of the user. The idea is that more and more user stories developed helps towards progressive evaluation. User stories do not handle the 'how to solve' question but rather addresses 'what is required' question. For each requirement a user stories is prepared in a clear and precise manner with a maximum of 15 user stories. The format of a user story includes a role, the goal and the reason. The format: As a <role> I want <goal/desire> in order to <receive/benefit. For example: As an author I want to write a good book in order to share my knowledge ------ ----------- I want to continue writing a good book................... We know 'why' the person is making the request. Following this path we want to cover the need as easily as we did in stating it. So the acceptance criteria are built the same way. Given <a role>, when <the action>, then <results>. Given writing a good book, as an author, I will be able to share my knowledge. User stories should be written in such a way so as to assign definite responsibility to the person from whom it has originated. It is understood by everybody, especially the one who needs it. The person who made them will be able to recognize their user story at any time in the development of the process.

Use cases: Use case and user stories can both be used in the methodology. Use cases **represent goals** that are achieved by an interaction of systems and devices. Each use case represents one goal. Eg: login to the website, click on the payments tab, pay the premium, receive the policy and pay for additional endorsements. In this manner, the functional requirements are mapped to use cases. Use cases are then mapped to test plans. They are represented by the systems modelling language (SysML). Given below is an illustration of use cases for Premium Payment.

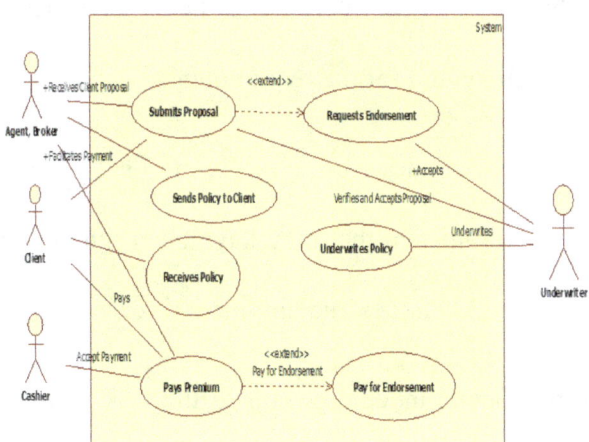

Note: Use cases are represented within the rectangular system boundary. (The above diagram has been drawn with the help of STAR UML.)

Use case document: The use case document has a **brief description of the functional requirements** and is included in the business requirement document. The document gives a rundown of the functions in all the applications and their overall relationship with each other. It also has a small index of the types of actors/users, their role and their access to the application. For example: User logs in with registered credentials; if correct then go to step '2'; otherwise go to 'account credentials' module

Product backlog: This represents the **consolidated user stories** for a requirement that is to be completed. It is taken as a measure of work during solution solicitation for the requirement.

Release notes: These describe what work has been **completed successfully**, the parameters that may have been ignored and what are to be done next to tackle issues and eliminate risks.

Scope modeling: Scope modeling refer to the task of **identifying** that what is needed or covered has been properly defined and captured. This enables the business processes to work synchronously with the needs of the organization.

Sequence diagrams give a **graphical representation** of interactions that can occur within the scope of business events. In fact, use cases are elaborated with the help of sequence diagrams. Given below is an illustration of a sequence diagram of possible scenarios when a customer requests an insurance policy.

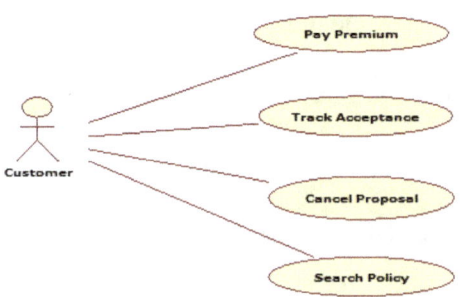

Sprint backlog: The sprint backlog represents the total user stories that are in the production environment. In other words, they indicate the **requirements that are presently being worked** upon for development. A maximum of 2 -3 weeks is given for a sprint to be developed.

Sprint status: The Agile team conducts daily meetings to discuss developments/work progress. The questions include what has been done yesterday, what is to be done today, what are the problem areas and constraints to achieving the goal.

Story points: Each team member/department of the team give their weightage about the complexity of the problem. Each user story

requirement is given weightage which determines the sequence in which functional parameters for the task are implemented.

Workflows: Work flows are activities that are initiated by events within or outside the organization. Workflows have a beginning and a terminal point and are designed from program to program level. Workflows management is rather done at **a process requirement level** instead of an individual level and document level. For example: A workflow begins with the agent who has collected a proposal from the customer. The workflow then passes on to the underwriting department where the proposal is accepted. The workflow again moves on to the accounts department to receive the premium and issue a receipt to the customer. The workflow ends when the receipt and the policy have been received by the customer.

Approval: Business requirements are mapped by the requirements documents. The requirements documents are designed to meet functional and non – functional requirements of the organization. The validated requirements documents are accepted and approved by all the **stakeholders**. The model is developed and monitored only after the approval by the stakeholders.

Client: They constitute the owners and end users of the system and are the ones who fund the development of the system. A **client contractual**

agreement is signed by the IT leader and the client after successful collaboration has been made, zeroing on the requirements of resources, time and costs.

Data Dictionary: These are made up of **standard definitions** and are uniform throughout the project. It should be identifiable and understood by the programmers and other stakeholders who need to refer to them. The primary elements are name, record, field and so on. The secondary data elements are made by sequencing, mathematical functions, and repetitions. These elements are the 'values and meanings' and are also called as 'attributes' which are tied with each other. Therefore the data dictionary enables cross references. Given below is an illustration of the data dictionary.

Field name	Description	Data type	Field size
insured_id		Autonumber	
agency_id	Close ended agents	Longinteger	
policy--_num		autonumber	

str_first_name	First Name	Text	200
str-_last_name	Last name	Text	200
str_DOB	Date	dd/mm/yy	35

Data Modelling: Data modelling addresses the data requirements of the problem statement. Data requirements are illustrated by the **'entity relationship diagram'** (ERD). The ERD is made to visually represent the interconnections between data of the 'entities'. The entity is a physical object or a place or a specific role. Example: customers, underwriting office, user, computer and so on. Each entity has specific pieces of related information or characteristics also called as 'attributes'. Attributes are named and have value and meanings and are contained in the data dictionary. Example: a policy has a name, date, category and risks. This 'metadata' is used for search and data categorization. Given below is an illustration of an ERD.

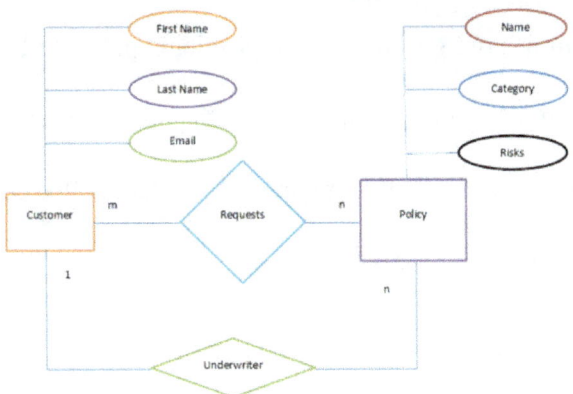

Elicitation Methods: Requirements are gathered by the process of elicitation. Other than simple observation about how things are working and how they ought to be working, there are various other methods of elicitation as well. The methods of elicitation include:

Brainstorming: This method requires participation from a group of stakeholders. The group may come up with different ideas and opinions about the proposed project. The brainstorming session should not be more than 30 minutes. All the ideas should be treated with equal importance and there should be no demarcation about whether an idea is good or bad. The next step is an analysis of the information. Once the analyses have been completed, the results should be informed on to all the participants. This is intended to encourage them to participate and attend future brainstorming sessions.

Crowdsourcing: This is an elicitation technique. Data and answers that are collected from a large group to solve problems prove to be more effective and innovative. The facts collected by this method are generally more substantial and correct when compared to the data collected from a smaller group of individuals.

Document Management: Document management starts at the beginning of the project. Being a primary source for elicitation, document management plays a crucial role in business process management. While collecting information from the documents, the analyst needs to be aware that officials within the organization may not be willing to reveal information. Hence, well-judged sources of information are selected by the analyst for eliciting information. Sources of information for document management in an organization are:

E mails

Letters

Reports

Transactions document

Finance and accounts documents

Technical department documents

Focus groups: This method serves to identify requirements too. Focus groups are formed by a set of heterogeneous participants consisting of different stakeholders. They present their opinion to the group moderator. The typical session lasts for around 3 to 4 hours. This serves as an effective method of elicitation as it allows for opinions from the participating stakeholders, which are tied to different solution sets.

Interviews: These have been the best source of qualitative information. The concerned stakeholders are contacted and relevant information to the project is sought to be elicited. For general information, a free and unstructured question answer session is enough. For specific information, a structured format of questions can be used. Unstructured format of questions elicit open ended responses which allows interviewees to tell whatever they want in their own words. The responses are interpreted by the interviewer who seeks to determine the type and the reasons why the information is being told. The interviewer also determines whether there are facts to support the information, whether any other relevant information is required and how the information can be put to use. The structured format however, elicits closed ended responses. The answers are elicited as specific choices, from which the interviewees have to choose, as required by the interviewer. Oftentimes, it may be difficult to obtain information from the stakeholders who may not be willing to part with information that is sensitive and confidential. Under such circumstances, tactical interviewing will be necessary.

Observation: Observing events as they happen gives first-hand information about activities, how document are processed and the specified course of events as they occur.

Prototyping: A sample of the product is made to elicit the feedback of the user. Generally, prototypes are made with technologies like additive manufacturing and 3D printing. Hence, prototyping becomes an economical method of elicitation. For insurance software, a sample layout of the pages or even an assimilation of use cases that provide the solution can be presented to the client to get their approval.

Requirements workshop: This is an event that involve key stakeholders and the subject matter experts. The workshop is facilitated by a team member who is neural to the outcome. Lasting for a period of two to three days, the workshop seeks to generate new ideas that are expressed as requirements. These types of requirements, including detailed ones are received and analyzed by the team members. After a detailed analysis has been made and the conclusions have been reached, a consensus about the final approach is reached among all the members of the workshop. All the requirements that are elicited in the workshop, as well as any outstanding issues, are recorded by a recorder who is also known as the scribe. The scribe maintains the minutes and records the proceedings of the workshop.

Seminars: A seminar has the participation of all the stakeholders and the IT team. This form of elicitation helps to collect relevant information and to strategize and plan what needs to be done.

Surveys and questionnaires: These methods of elicitation save on time, cost and money. However they are to be carefully designed so as to be relevant and effective. Open ended questionnaire allow the respondents to express their own opinion and answers. Close ended questionnaires are straight jacketed and allow controlled responses according to the options provided in the questionnaire.

-----------------*End of elicitation methods*-------------

Enduring and volatile requirements: Some requirements that were thought as stable or enduring may require a change or alteration. Requirement changes or modifications are managed by a useful routine known as continuous **process mapping**.

Game Theory: Decision making is one of the basic activities of human being. However, decisions cannot be made without a basis. Many a times, decisions are based on the reaction of others. The intentions of others play a very important role. These 'others' are called as the 'players' in game theory. Motivations are based on the payoffs in decision making. The outcomes are ultimately determined by payoffs. Working together and cooperation is better than working without cooperation. This is what the game theory highlights.

Glossary: There are abbreviations and acronyms used in the business operations. The document terms are unique to the project. They pertain to the domain and enable cross reference.

Organization – roles – interfaces – boundaries - requirements standards: An organization is structured to accomplish some purpose and objectives. Specific skills and responsibilities are needed for this purpose and are known as the 'roles'. Roles define the work packages and their relationships with one another. The junctures where work packages are received by a unit of communication or delivered to other units of communication are known as 'boundaries'. 'Interfaces' refer the correlation of activities at some point of time, when boundaries of work packages come close to each other. For all of these, the work packages have specific requirements which have minimum quality standards.

Records perusal: Records can help in estimating the volume of transactions and data storage requirements. Most organizations have written guides, policy manuals and standard operating procedures. These form a good source of information and can give an idea about what the system constitutes. In an Insurance company, the policy guides and manuals can define the design and constraints of the system. The other documents are the premium register, claims disbursement reports, management expenses report, commission and bonus report, surveyors and investigators report.

Requirements review: Once the requirements document has been prepared, the preferred course of action is to know whether the document has been made clearly and accurately. This is done by bringing together all the stakeholders to go through the document, to point out mistakes and loopholes and to make further suggestions. Requirements review improves the quality of the requirements document. It also establishes the accuracy and prevents wastage of resources, time and cost in the event that a wrong idea has been implemented.

Requirements validation: Requirements validation is made to get the approval of the stakeholders. This is done after the requirements have been gathered, prioritized and organized. The requirements documents are referred to the users to verify whether this is actually what they need. The recommendation of all the stakeholders can again be noted. If any changes are required to be done, the requirements document can be revised, organized and prioritized. This will enable the accomplishment of objectives of all the stakeholders, while at the same time saves on cost and time at a later date. The techniques for requirements validation with stakeholders include (a) Stakeholder's approval of the documents and/or (b) Stakeholder's approval of prototype.

Scenarios and use cases: Scenarios and use case represents the manner in which the 'goal' and the 'processes' work together. Scenarios denote the sequence of actions that the 'actor' should do to achieve a specific goal. Hence, a scenario describes the *approach* to arriving at the solution. However this one approach may not be the only one. For example: Premium can be collected by the underwriting manager who collects a check for premium payment in the office and enter the details with a keyboard. Alternatively, premium can be collected by an agent, a broker or a distribution agent who enters the details via a mobile or a computer keyboard online elsewhere, which is verified by the underwriter. Otherwise, premium may also be paid online by clients/customers, which is verified by the underwriter. We understand now that scenarios correspond to the sequence of steps that the actor does to complete a task to achieve the goal. Scenarios may have some preconditions and post conditions to take place. *Preconditions:* A precondition is something that is necessary for the scenario to take place and is likely when we need a scenario or use case to take place. For example: The user must be logged in to make an online payment. *Post conditions:* Corresponds to what should happen after the scenario has reached the end. For example: Once the premium has been paid, the receipt should automatically attach to the policy docket/file.

Use cases are much more comprehensive and are meant to manage the scenarios. And hence, use cases describe the simplest way of achieving a goal using various approaches and components. They also describe the number of ways that an actor can interrelate or respond to the given situation to accomplish one or more of the 'goals'. Each use case represents one goal. Eg: login to the website, click on payments tab, pay the premium, receive the policy and pay for additional endorsements. There is standard primary flow which is the normal course of action. There could also be secondary flows which are alternative courses of action. For example: login to the website, select the product, click on agents tab, select the agent, pay premium with agents code and receive e – policy. The actions that comes from the primary flows or any other another alternative flows are all described by use cases. Use case describes the simplest way to accomplish the goals represent all the possible types of interactions between the user and the system. Hence, they also serve as a source to get a clear and short description about the specific outcome of an application/product. Undoubtedly, the role that is performed by the 'actor' to achieve a goal could be performed by possible combinations of use cases. This relationship between use cases and actors are known as 'associations'.

Structured and form based language specifications: Clarity, efficiency and flexibility in expressions of requirements is successfully enabled by the structured natural language. For system designs, structured natural language lays emphasis on procedures. They specify the functions of entities, provide the description of inputs and the description of outputs, the applicable pre –conditions and post – conditions and the impacts that they have, if any. In some events structured natural language is supported by forms and visual approach.

SWOT analysis: A requirements document can include a review of the strengths, weaknesses, opportunities and threats of an organization. During the review, some processes can be given more weightage while some others can be altered or eliminated. Benchmarking is a tool used in SWOT analysis. It is used to compare the strengths and weaknesses of the organization against its peers and competitors. Benchmarks are made to set standards of costs, quality, time and service standards. Benchmarking enables effective analysis during solution solicitation.

System user and domain requirements: System and domain requirements are described and written to form the basis of the contract between the client and the customer. It should explain the mandatory resources required for the system.

Tools for documentation: BizAgi Modeller, Asure RP, Axure, Visio and word excel JIRA are good applications for good user interface and security of data,

Exercises

(1) Jot down some parameters about requirements for your industry and for your organization.

(2) Do a requirements gathering exercise for your organization.

Hint: Use the following steps:

- *Identify the features of the existing business system and development constraints.*

- *List the specifications given by the end users/the customers.*

- *Review the products that the organization needs.*

- *The reasons why the product is required.*

- *Jot down the needs unfulfilled by the existing system of documentation.*

- *Describe of the final product and foresee constraints.*

- *Describe of the services to be completed successfully.*

- *Note down, classified and prioritized the requirements.*

- *Check that these requirements are designed to make plans that work towards finding a solution statement.*

- *Prioritize requirements along with other project documents.*

- *Elicitate data from existing business documents and from key personnel*

- *Collect and analyze data.*

- *Create a draft version of the document after the requirements have been identified, classified and prioritized.*

- *Put up the proposed document for review and recommendations to several competent authorities including the end –users, developers, project managers and other*

- *Forward the completed requirements reports to the authorities concerned for a final decision.*

THE SYSTEM

'A system is a set of interacting or interdependent component parts forming a complex/intricate whole'; Wikipedia the Free Encyclopedia.

Designing a system calls for arranging and accessing information and data to suit the requirements of the entity. It becomes imperative that every single possible transaction and event that could arise should be taken into consideration. Exceptional situations also should be identified and at the same time, methods of dealing with exceptional situations should also be included. For all these reasons, system development is often the toughest part in the development of the IT department.

As the system is made up of a number of programs, the problems need to be wholly analyzed. A step by step solution is sought by logical sequencing and coding of the data which are represented by UML enabled DFD's. For this, the Functional Specification and Requirement Specifications document is prepared and validated and is often referred to for guidance.

Identifying exceptional situations is very important because a computer does not have intuitive and judgmental capacities. Instead, the computer uses programmed logic by breaking down the solution finding into a series of discrete steps and functions with the help of DFD's and coding. An example of an exceptional situation: Given that final claim payable = Gross claims – Deductibles. Suppose the gross claims work out to $225/- while the standard deduction is $250/-. It is obvious to the claims adjuster that the claim is not payable. However, if this situation is not recognized by the computer, the software estimates the claim as $ -25 and print out a check for $ -25. This type of situation occurs when the system analyst who designed the process has not correctly planned the response that the computer was expected to give. Undoubtedly, solutions can be formulated after all such exceptional situations are identified and included.

The 'platform' and language implementation of the software is decided. For example: Java platform, Silverlight, .NET framework, Oracle database, Linux. They are mainly constituted by Relation Data Based Management Systems, the Front End Tools for coding and the Operating System.

System Specifications

Files Used

#Mode of using files

File naming conventions

File design

Screen layouts

Reports layout

Sequence of process

File sharing methods

Design menu tree

Design each menu

Assign codes

Set system controls

Methods for system analysis and design

SSAD: SSAD or 'Structured Systems Analysis and Design' can be used for analyzing and get amazing systems rolling. SSAD and Unified Modelling Language (UML), which enable graphic designing, provide methods for systems designing. DFD's constitute an important perspective of SSAD. DFD's are diagrammatic presentation of the system made in the form of flow charts. *History:* DFD's were first invented by Larry Constantine during 1975. The UML was first developed by Grady Booch, Ivar

Jacobson and Rambaugh, during 1994 -96 at Rational Software (which has been acquired by IBM during 2003). SSAD was developed in UK during 1980 – 81, by Learmonth Burchett Management Systems and the Central Computer Telecommunications Agency.

Coding: The 'platform' has front end tools to enable coding. The function of coding is to get an accurate specification about the systems intended routine. They are formulated within the programs and define input/output formats, file layouts and processing logic. The coding system will use meaningful data names; include a commentary in a simple and straightforward layout.

Systems Designing:

The Insurance industry models that are popularly used include IBM IIA and ACCORD mainframes. Whatever the model being used, an analysis is made of the existing manual system before process designs are made. The objective is to set up an *online front office operating system* to manage the day to day transactions with the help of networking. Networking enables computer systems at the same/ different places to be interconnected for effective communication and remote activities. For example: a divisional offices' transactions and accounting data are submitted online to their head office at the end of each day, an insurance agent accepts a credit card payment at customers household.

The programs can be developed using a chosen, compatible and preferred interacting computer language. For example Java platform, Silverlight, .NET framework, Oracle database, Linux, Windows API. Also needed are an HTTP server, a backend database (that is made of tables and help retrieve information and store data), and a hypertext processor (that can administer the backend database over the world wide internet). The organization may have some preferences, including Sparx Enterprise Architect, JIRA, Blue works, Blue prints, Waterfall model, Agile model, which can be used along with a combination of Excel, Word, Visio, SharePoint, OneNote and MS office.

Touchstones

Business Rules: Business rules make up the 'rules engine'. Business rules govern the workflow pattern when marking business processes. Examples of business rules: (1) A claim that is above $1000/- is subject to deductible of $250/-. (2) A policy that has premium over $2000/- per annum will be categorized as a special client policy. New business rules may be added in the 'rules engine'. They determine policies and procedures and also provide the framework for the required business process automation. The rules based approach is of primary importance as it addresses the scope and needs of particular processes.

Data modeling: This is the process of sequencing the data to meet the requirements of business processes. Business logistics determine the sequence in data: Rules (----determine-------) Activities (------- determine -----------) Business Processes (----- determine --------) Creation of happenings or events. Typical scenarios are logically sequenced for programs. For example: The payroll module program has data of the names and employee number. The module connects this data with the data of salary payable, calculates salary, prints the payroll details and enables salary payment to the employees. The tax module program then connects the payroll data, calculates tax, deducts from the annual salary at the end of the financial year and submits the returns.

Notations:

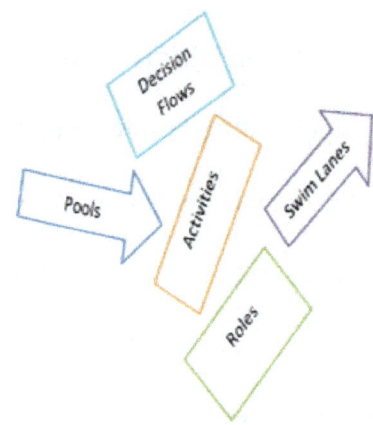

A uniform interrelated set of notations are used to standardize business processes. XML process definition language or BPMN business process modeling notation may be used throughout the project.

Process development tools: Grapholite and Ludichart can be accessed anywhere, anytime. Yed is a free processing mapping tool and supports business process mapping.

Recap: The system analyst has the prime and foremost and at the same time the most difficult work to do to enable automation and needs to understand what is required. Understand the problems that have to be cleared away to meet the requirements. Analyze every single possibility that could happen. Identify exceptional situations. Decide on what action should be taken in case an exceptional situation occurs. Write down all the plausible steps to the solution that can solve the problem. Descriptive instructions may become impractical and cumbersome to follow. The use of a flow – chart can is definite and effective. A flow –chart gives the diagrammatic representation of the logical and sequential steps for arriving at the solution. The flows - chart however, have its limitations and cannot be used for complex solution finding. For example; setting up a front office system with the accounting module merged with underwriting and claims module may require complex program logic, in which case the flow chart becomes complex and difficult to follow. For this purpose the analyst makes use of Structured System Analysis and Design.

The system development life cycle

A system life cycle is associated with every system. Human beings and all living thing have a life cycle of birth, growth, maturity, death and rebirth. Similarly, the computer also has a system life cycle. The system development life cycle (SDLC) forms the 'model' like the waterfall model or the iterative model or the agile model. The SDLC gives a way for the activities of software development to be divided into determined activities that are done one after another or done at the same time. Activities of the software department may also overlap one another. This done so that the software developed is of high quality which meets the requirements. The life cycle of a computer system is associated with the following framework:

Define initial requirements and plan the layouts: Requirements are elicited from the users. The requirements could include searching for insurance products in the website, enabling a customer login and agent login, enabling an online payment mode, having only 10 functionalities on the home screen, and some administrative functionality in the website and the like. All the requirements are analyzed and documented.

The system design: This is a high level design of the system. It determines the data structure; about whether the system will use the database or data from web services. The other major constituents of system design are the individual modules including the policy module, accounting module, claims module, investment module, coinsurance and reinsurance module, HRM module, customer service module and the major reports required. System designs are also constituted by the entity relationship diagram. The entities in an insurance company are defined to include the visitors to the website, the customers in the website, the products and customer's orders.

Draw the program design by coding: Coding is done by the developers according to the software architecture that has been designed. A major task in coding is the integration of units according to the system specifications. To enable this integration, the data flow, data access, data logic and the user interface are directed by the code. Codes also enable error messages. The finalized output of coding is the software.

Enable testing: The developers test the logic of their functions for each and every unit. For example, the underwriting unit should print a policy once the proposal is recorded as approved and the premium is recorded as received.

Enable integration and installing: The focus is on testing the integration between the units. For example, the premium received in the underwriting unit should reflect in the accounting unit. Then the system testing is done according to the system specifications for which test cases are made. Modifications are done in an iterative manner until the system becomes accurate and correct.

Routine and non – routine maintenance are done for smooth functioning and to prevent major breakdowns. Working within this framework makes it easy to monitor the life – cycle of the computer system. It also enables the management to assess the resources that are needed at every stage of development.

A continuous assessment is made for activities, events, processes and components that have not been taken into consideration. The ongoing project is monitored and the progression measured by metrics and key performance indicators. Metrics and KPI's are indicators that are made. They are used to measure the level of progress in achieving a certain goal. They serve as tools to monitor and evaluate progress. They track the progress toward the intended goals, the efficacy of a solution and the usefulness of inputs and outputs.

Typical technology metrics and KPI's: Uptime, *Speed* and Accuracy.

Typical process metrics and KPI's: Customer satisfaction rating, Average handle time, Average wait time.

Typical performance metrics and KPI's: Policy sales growth, Renewals and new policies, Incurred claims and loss ratio, Revenue growth.

Exercises

Ponder on a systems design for your organization, whichever sector of the economy it is. Estimate the difficulties and constrains of the present system.

Draw an outline systems design outlay for your organization.

Hint: You can download and use the following tool called STAR UML.

At this stage, you can click on 'analysis model' and 'design model' and go ahead and practice.

Scenario 1: An artist needs to complete the practice work and art work. The assignments are challenging and difficult to achieve. Besides, the artist spends time on self-improvement activities like music and tennis and volleyball. The artist also requires sufficient funds to carry on all these activities. What is going to be the time and cost schedule to complete all the activities? How are the efforts going to be streamlined to be able to match with the budget and objectives?

Scenario 2: An insurance company needs to incorporate a new endorsement within its Motor policy. The business already has its software system set up. The inclusion of an endorsement meant affecting entries in the underwriting and claims settlement modules. Besides it will require expertise, time and expenses.

In both the scenarios, activities are done to reach the objectives within the time and cost constraints. A set of activities that works to complete a task makes a process and undoubtedly, all individuals and entities follow some processes to complete tasks.

Processes

As understood, activities that are logically ordered to complete tasks are called processes. Processes differ between organizations and there is no right or wrong. Processes are affected by many external factors including the market and political climate of the country. Well-designed business process can be considered as assets.

Process Modelling

Historical data about business operations which are the 'as-is' processes, are descriptive and statistical in nature. They are often referred to make more effective processes in the future. For the 'to-be' situation to come about there may be a requirement for additional resources and techniques. This transition also known as 'process transformation', ushers in a more efficient and effective way of working.

The upgradation of business processes is better done as a collaborative venture that involves both the business unit and IT people. Initially, the requirements are gathered and the business requirements documents are finalized. Then the current processes are redesigned according to the recommendations in the business requirements documents. Updating current processes will require real time monitoring. Real time monitoring is made possible by key process indicators or KPI's. KPI's include comparing the planned and actual time involved, costs incurred, progress and quality of the outcomes.

Processes are unraveled by discovery diagrams and process modelling. Process modelling begins with the evaluation of the company needs as in the requirements documents. An analysis is made about the work that is done, taking into consideration the 'w' of work – 'where', 'why', 'when', 'by whom' and 'who' is responsible. Taking all this into consideration, a good amount of time, effort, ideation and significant investment are needed to create and implement a new business process. The new processes are also likely to introduce new roles. Some questions considered when determining processes include:

What are the factors that increase consumer satisfaction?

What factors improve efficiency and profits?

What processes can be altered or changed?

What processes have well defined obstacles to change?

Which process can add value to the business?

Which processes can be implemented quickly and efficiently?

Determine what could best be done in the situation.

Elements of a Process

A typical business process have the following constituents: (a) start of events (b) logically connecting tasks (c) the routines and (d) the subroutines for completing the task.

The work flows in business processes are determined sequentially. The step by step sequencing of work flows not only gives the direction of the work flows, but also helps to trace the path of processes. Processes are generally described by means of notation. Notations and data flow diagrams are used to identify and plot the path of the process.

Drawing the insurance underwriting processes

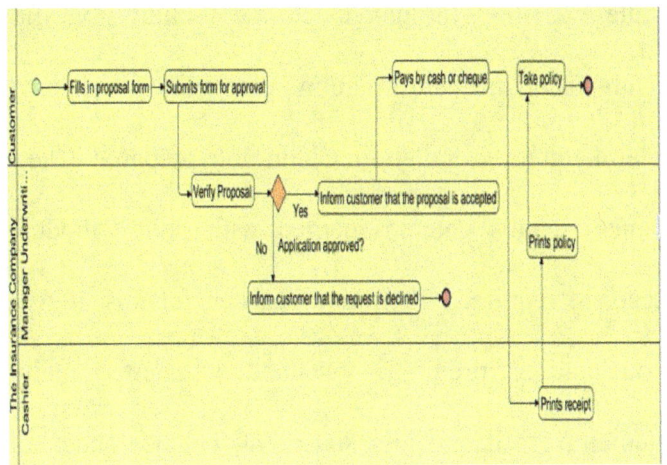

Tools to create business processes

Visio, smartdraw, HTML and MS Paint are tools that can be used for diagrams and for detailed markings. A quick and easy to use online tool is called 'gliffy' which is an online diagram and flowchart tool. Another one is 'bezagi' which allows more mapping in a less cluttered manner and also tells you whether the flow of logic is correct or not. Visual paradigm gives an application development platform.

An umbrella of insurance processes

Customer fills in proposal form and submits to agent/at the underwriting office. Proposal perused and checked whether there is insurance already existing for the same risk. Proposal accepted with/without specified terms and conditions. Receipt of premium recorded in underwriting and accounts module. A policy docket is formed with coinsurance and reinsurance details. The data is linked to the MIS module and investment module and claim module. Claims Intimated. Policy validity verified. Claims documents obtained and information entered. Claim payment after approval. Claim amount calculation. Claim note prepared. Check prepared. Claims payment details entered merged with policy module and MIS module. Records required: Premium register, claims register, prepaid premium, outstanding premium, outstanding claims, claim reserves, income statement, profit and loss statement, balance sheet, management expenses, budget performance on a weekly, monthly half yearly and yearly basis. Tax returns, employee benefits, employee payroll. Data from underwriting claims and office expenses and accounts modules analyzed. Accurate reports generated.

Touchstones

Actors: Actors have particular roles and they work in referred situations. They are assigned *unique names* which are listed within the business rules. The actors have to perform specific actions – which are given in the verb form. For example in an insurance company: The *underwriter* peruses, verifies and approves proposals and underwrites the policy. The *claims adjuster* verifies the claim intimation form and other claim documents and then processes the claim according to rules and regulations.

Actual process: The actual process refers to data access, modification, rearrangement, deletion and cumulative accumulation for getting a required response or output. The actual processes made possible by EDP, are defined by the programs that have been designed and implemented according to the requirements documents.

Algorithm: This refers to a simple language which forms a mode of instruction with the computer. They prepare a sequential order for a series of instructions that are required to perform specified operations.

Associations: These show the relationship between the use cases and the actor. For example: An underwriter (actor) logs into the system and is authenticated, uses keyboard to fill in proposal details, uses some keyboard functions to verify policy details aspects, uses keyboard functions to access coinsurance, reinsurance, MIS and receipt module, uses keyboard and printer to print the policy, logs out of the system (use cases). A claims adjuster (actor) logs into the system and is authenticated, uses keyboard to fill in claim details, uses some key board function to link to underwriting module and claims master to verify claims, uses keyboard functions to prepare claims settlement statement, uses keyboard functions to send claims settlement statement to accounting department giving claims payable details, logs out of the system (use cases).

Business process model and notation(BPMN): This a popular form of graphical representation of business models, which have been recently developed and maintained by the Business Process Management Institute and the Object Management Group. They not only provide a standard notation that is understood by all stakeholders, but also provide an interface between the graphics and the business process execution language (BPEL). The four basic elements are: (1) 'Events' (start, intermediate and end) which are represented by circles (2) 'Activities' (tasks, sub –process, calls and transactions) which are represented by rounded corner rectangles Different organizations are represented as 'pools'. The functions and roles are classified as 'lanes' within the pools. (3) 'Gateways' which are represented by diamond shapes (these are used to fork and merge the activity flow depending on the requirement) (4) 'Connections' are represented by solid, dashed and dotted lines (they connect the events, activities and gateways using sequences, messages and associations). In addition to the 'elements', more information is provided by the developers in the form of 'artifacts' comprised of (a) 'data – objects' in activities, other autonomous (b) 'groups' of activities and (c) 'annotations' that give a clear explanation of the model/diagram. An example of business process activities in insurance is given below. The diagram has been constructed using 'visual paradigm'. You can consider using 'visual paradigm' for practice.

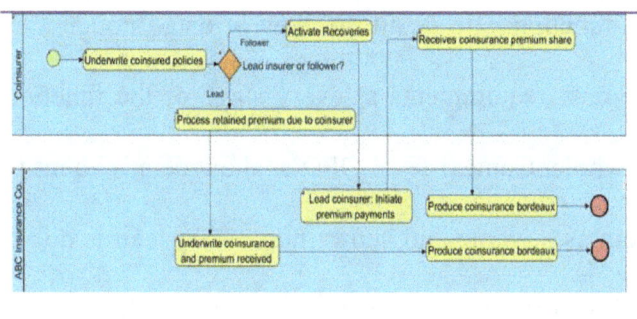

Business rules management system: Rules exist and the employees may or may not be aware that they are following them. Business rules are defined, analyzed and managed. They can be clearly understood, changed, altered and reused to manage and maintain the decision logic flow requirements. Business rules are generally contained in the business rules journal. For example: Policy is valid after realization of premium. Structural rules are based on if – then scenario and help determine whether it is true or not. For example: If premium has been paid for the proposal, then the policy is verified, approved and issued. If the premium is paid during office hours, then the insurance cover starts immediately. Operative rules govern actions. For example: Once a policy commences, the company is liable to honor claims made by the insured. Some rules are flexible and change within processes. For example: Annual premium payment mode can be changed to premium payment on a yearly, half yearly or annual basis.

Data Flow Diagrams: They form an important perspective in SSAD and make a diagrammatic presentation of the system in the form of flow charts. DFD's main function is to detail the flow of data through a system. They illustrate the data requirements at every stage of the functionality of the system as a whole. Context level DFD's, show details about the data flow for the system as a whole and shows how the system is divided into sub-processes. Similarly, process level DFD's traces the data flow through processes. Though the representations are unique by themselves, they are useful for setting up alternate paths for the process. DFD's also helps establish the requirements of internal data storage for construction of the system and processes.

Data flows: Data flows are comprised of packets of information flow that are sequenced by arrows. Data flows are made by naming the data and labeling the arrows that connect them.

Enterprise Process Management: EPM is concerned with integration of activities within the organization. EPM is essential for organizing the all the factors constituting the system. It also serves as an instrument of control and monitors the progress of the system. The factors constituting the EPM are given below:

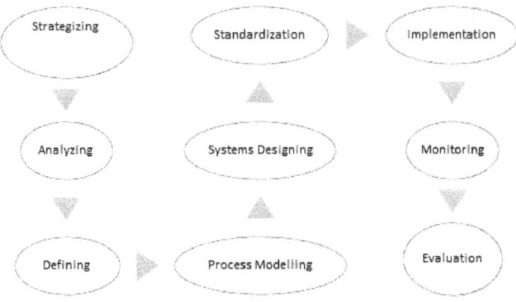

External entities: These are objects outside the system with which it communicates. For example: potential clients and government portals. These boundaries form the sources and destination of the systems inputs and outputs.

Flow chart: It is a diagrammatic representation of the processes to follow which draw the logic paths contained within a computer program. A step by step representation is made possible with the use of certain elements that includes the start/stop box, the process box which also allows arithmetic operations, the input – output box and the decision box. The chart contains directional arrows which represent the transfer of 'command' (and not data as in DFD's) between the elements (which include the start/stop box, the process box which also allows arithmetic operations, the input – output box and the decision box). The flow chart also has a connector to connect two different parts of the flow chart.

Name: For a process to be made, the interrelated work and document flow have a naming convention that is used.

Illustration

#Underwriting process

#Claims process

#Approve proposal

#Finalize claim

#Customer pays premium

Pay agency commission

#Salary computation

Reinsurance process

Process analysis: The study provides an understanding of the existing processes and the organizations goals and activities. The parameters considered here are the inputs and outputs of processes, the roles of the employees and the suppliers and the consumers. Process analysis suggests means to arrive at scalability and improve resource utilization by identifying the areas of improvement. UML tools are helpful for process analysis. UML tools enable graphical diagram that give the order and sequences of processes. They are helpful to manage and logically configure processes and also identify exceptions to the normal course of events.

Process designs: Process designs are made to create the 'software artifact' that the user requires. The business requirements documents establish how the business should be redesigned for work. The specifications are captured by the process design like the hypothetical one illustrated below.

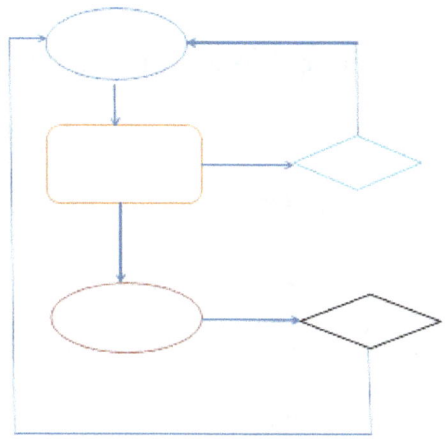

Process designs are designed, implemented and managed within the platform or outside the platform which the project is working. Process designs are simple UML based flow charts and are run on a graphic organizer or a 'storyboard'. They can be used to trace and analyze the effects of process changes to the existing business system.

Process maturity curve: Introducing new roles and processes into a business depends on the ability or maturity of the organization to withstand new processes and changes. Until the goal is reached, processes may need to be filtered into the existing system because the short run internal capabilities may not be sufficient to withstand new process.

Process transformation: Process transformation occurs due to improvements which could be very intricate and of a large scale. Moreover, process changes will cause a change in the way work is being done. This causes 'impacts' made to the elements of a process. We already know that the elements of a process are constituted by (a) start of events (b) logically connecting tasks (c) the routines and (d) the subroutines for completing the task. Impacts on elements of the processes can be traced by the 'as is – to be' process diagrams. Let us take a hypothetical example of the coinsurance of ABC Insurance Co: The 'as –is' situation is drawn for ABC Insurance company when there was no specific accounting department in the process diagram. The 'to – be' process diagram is drawn for the situation when there is a distinct accounting department. So instead of just the premium Bordeaux, ABC Insurance Company also prints the premium receipt and the discharge voucher when the accounting department is included in the process diagram.

The 'as is' process diagram for ABC Insurance Co:

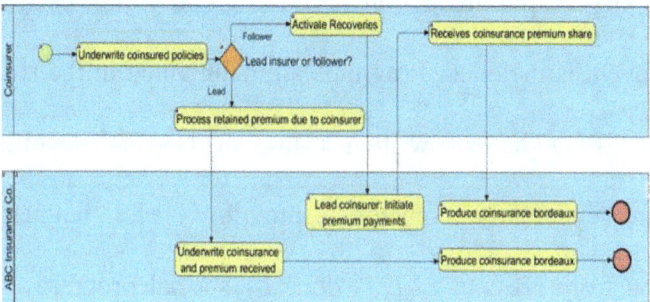

The 'to – be' process diagram of ABC Insurance Co:

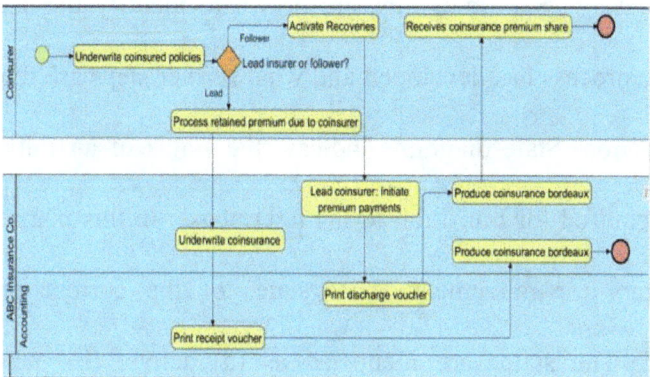

Programming: Programs are instructions given to the computer. These are the input – output instructions. To design programs, each and every possible event is included. Programs are maintained in the storage area within the CPU. They are written in low level or high level languages which are eventually converted into low level languages. The conversion from HLL to LLL is done by special programs known as interpreters and compilers.

State diagrams: State diagrams are drawn to identify the stage up to which the process has developed and what further steps are required for its completion. State diagrams indicate the status of an initiative and what is required for transition to the next phase. In this manner, it sets the triggers for movement. The 'state' of the current process is identified. The states are identified as (a) active, (b) pending, (c) paused, (d) cancelled, (e) failed and (f) finished. For identifying the 'state' of the process, relevant information is collected from persons in senior management as they are accountable in the future.

The decision management programs: Well drawn business processes serve as assets and are a means to fulfill the requirements of the user. The decision management programs for business processes are based on two software technologies concepts: *(1) Business event processing system:* Business processes of the organization are designed according to specific work activities paths and business rules. As activities take place some implications or events are created. Example: policy underwritten, premium received, claims intimation, claims paid and so on. A number of events occur in business operations every day. An event can start and can happen over a period of time. For example, a claim reported at one time and settled some time later. Business events are complex and occur in a random order and have no definite time to happen. The events could cause more activities to start or could be completed by ongoing activities. Events can be linked within and between departments. *(2) Business process management:* BPM is about analyzing and designing processes for end to end work. BPM is concerned with what, where, why and by whom the work is done. BPM also considers roles of the persons/actors and their responsibilities. BEP and BPM are together used to design the decision making programs. (BEP and BPM can be designed by a tool called 'visual paradigm'. You can google it and use it for practice.)

The event planning solution inter relates the pattern of events. This is done to achieve the best reasoning and logical order. In this manner, many interconnected events can be made to work together with greater efficiency. For example, when a claim has occurred in an insurance policy and is entered as a record, the premium payment particulars are connected. The events may take place at a specific moment in time. For example: collection of a check or cash for premium payment. Events may take place over a period of time. For example: The time take for processing claims. Nowadays, with the use of graphical user interface, business event planning solutions can be made without having to know about programming in IT. Business process management (BPM) and business event planning (BEP) solutions work in harmony. It is important to illustrate the numerous associations between the actors and use – cases which require specific preconditions and post conditions. You can consider using 'visual paradigm' for practice.

Exercises

Identify and draw business processes in your organizations. Assign event and roles for the activities.

Hint

Business process analysis needs creativity and analytical thinking abilities.

In-depth knowledge of the situation is needed.

A feasibility study can then help determine which solution works best.

Once the need has been identified, business process requirements need to be drawn in relation to data.

These requirements need to be traced to the constraints of cost, time and quality.

The problems of the situation should have to be solved expediently.

Relevant technology to be identified for successful launch of the requirements.

The problem solving process and the solution should fall within the strategy, mission and vision set by the company.

Metrics and KPI's

Metrics and Key Process Indicators are used for monitoring progress. They measure the performance of the 'solution processes' towards fulfilling the objectives of the stakeholders. In other words, it compares how the specifications (example: underwriting premium, claims payments, accounts and investments module and compliance module), features (example: RDBMS, automatic backup of data, accessible by PC and mobile, user interface, customer interface, user login, client login, agent login) and performance standards (example: speed, capacity, security and reliability) have been implemented as against the results expected of it.

Typical technology metrics and KPI's:

Uptime	Reliability
Speed	Capacity
Accuracy	Strength
Compliance	Testability
Availability	Learnability

Typical process metrics and KPI's:

Customer rating

Effectiveness

Efficiency

Average handle time

Average wait time

Average turnover

Typical performance metrics and KPI's:

Policy sales growth
Renewals ratio
Incurred claims ratio
Revenue growth

KPI's are popularly represented by the 'balanced scorecard'. A 'balanced scorecard' is made by setting benchmarks for standards to be achieved. KPI's indicate the level of progress achieved by correlating the performance towards the benchmarks. They track the progress toward the intended goals, the efficacy of a solution and the usefulness of inputs and outputs.

96

	Benchmark 1	Benchmark2	Benchmark 3	Benchmark 4	Benchmar5
Finance	X		0		X
Customer Relations		X	X	0	
Operations	x	X			0
Marketing			0	x	X

'X' is denoted when benchmark has been realized.

'0' is denoted when benchmark has not been realized.

QC in processes:

When processes are to be transformed, all the elements of the process are remodeled and regulated. The remodeling is done to makes changes and improvements to the 'as –is' processes. The 'as –is' processes are the touchstones to measure progress, improvements and upgrades. Even a single process improvement is rarely made in one step. Rather, new inductions and continuous improvements are effectuated step by step. Follow – up is especially needed with any approach which allows for changes to be included strategically and not just for short term gains. Continuous process improvement requires optimization at any one point of time and so the suboptimal and broken processes that cause bottlenecks are rectified. Hence, the knowledge of processes followed by the current employees and their experience will prove to be helpful to get an overall perspective about the existing situation. As processes are being redesigned, progress and improvements are tracked. Here are some examples of process tracking:

Underwriting processing time reduced by 75%

Claims processing time reduced by 60%

Interlinking between claims and underwriting data made successfully.

Costs cut as planned; profitability has increased by 30%.

Online mode has been set up and running profitably.

Key Process Indicators (KPI) handling being done.

Quality management

A stitch in time saves nine. Quality assurance does involve cost, time and patience, but at the same time enables accuracy and reduces wasted efforts.

Techniques:

Deming cycle: Developed by Dr W Edward Deming, this technique makes use of the following functions: PLAN the events and model, DO work upon the model and let it happen, CHECK periodically to control the directions of the operations and ACT upon what is required to be done at that moment. Plan – Do – Check charts are developed to enable regulation of quality. It can be observed that when this principle is practiced, then a continuous process improvement becomes ingrained within the model.

Six Sigma: The six sigma model was developed by Saki chi Toyota. The model formed one of the elements of the Toyota Production System. It is one of the basic tools of quality measurement. Also called 'lean manufacturing', the technique seeks to find out the root cause of the problem. The next step in this method provides for ensuring the systematic updating and correction of processes. This is done well in time so that the model can perform flawlessly. The Motorola model during 1986 sought to obtain 99.99996% accuracy using the six sigma technique.

SIPOC model: Extending the Plan, Do and Control model, this model was developed by Peter Scholtes during 1988. The model was compiled in his work called 'The team handbook'. In this model, the organization is described in terms of the following components: Suppliers, Input, Process, Output, Customers. When described in this manner, it becomes possible to discover and plug the loopholes and constraints faced by the organization. This model was used in total quality management during the 1980's. Nowadays its use is found in the Six Sigma processes.

Pareto diagrams: This technique was introduced by Vilfredo Pareto during 1906, which made an interesting observation about the relative importance of some factors which included supplies and customers. According to Pareto's findings 80% of organizations process constraints will be due to 20% of the inputs from the suppliers. Similarly, 80% of the profits are bound to originate from 20% of the customers.

Statistical techniques: Statistical techniques that are harnessed for total quality management include histograms, causation and correlation analysis and scatter diagrams. They explain a lot about the production processes and give a feedback about managerial performance.

Feedback: Questions about service can be addressed to customers. What are the services being provided? What services need to be provided? What services are being done exceptionally well? What services are not being done well at all? What should be done? What processes should be discontinued? What processes should be continued?

Ideation: This technique allows the team to come up with all sorts of ideas. A gamut of ideas are invited which include not just ideas that are practical, but also ideas which are not so practical; some stupid ideas; some good ideas and some brilliant ideas too. At this stage, the objective is to gather as much quantity and not quality. Therefore, at this stage judgments about the ideas are not made. Just having lots of ideas help generate more ideas. In this process of ideation, the ideas multiply as more ideas are brought forward. Ultimately, effective ideas are generated.

Idea Webbing: Participants are made to handle the responsibility of collecting information and findings before they bring their ideas into the next group meeting. The brainstorming session follows next, during the group meeting. This enables the quick and easy assimilation of information from participants. This process of information gathering enables effective decision making. For example: when working towards creating a marketing module, the management should decide whether the company needs an incentive scheme for their underwriting agents? Are incentives necessary? Can the company afford it? How should costs and benefits weigh? What if there are varying minimum threshold of premium collection and so on. These are all connected and the participants volunteer to work on the topic of their choice and submit their research findings at the next meeting.

Problem tracking: Once the objective has been identified and a possible solution to the problem statement is developed and quality management sets in, then the problem tracking is done. Problem tracking includes identifying elements that measure the step by step performance and repercussions of the solution. In the event that the solution is not effective, the problem should be traced to a much nobler and philosophical goal. The five whys' approach could be used to find the main cause of the problem: Why was the technique used? Why was it not satisfactory? Why do we need to know more about the efficacy? Why the root cause of constraint has been part of the technique? A renewed path for rejuvenation of the situation is explained. Alternatively, diagrams giving the cause and effect relationship, also called Ishikawa diagrams, could be made use of for solving the situation. This is important as it helps to handle situational constraints as and when they arise.

Exercises

Identify some constraints in the business processes within your organization.

Suggest some processes to overcome these constraints.

The methods in the product development and knowledge about the insurance domain are essential at every stage. They are relevant even during the stage of testing the product.

The ultimate product is the outcome of several stages of development and problem solving. The system is tested once the product has been developed. This process is a critical one and may take a greater part of the budget. During this process, the program is run with the sole intention of finding errors and causes of the program failures. Problem solving for program failures should be considered as part of the final product and as an opportunity to work upon and improve the present situation.

Solutions: Solutions, as we have known, are solicited to meet the user requirements. These solutions have to be tracked and measured as and when they are implemented. When solutions are not optimizing goals then alterations and alternative solutions are taken into consideration. Even then the alterations and alternatives that do not work may need to be eliminated. Solution soliciting is crucial and will be done as ongoing improvements.

Continuous improvement: If problems remain unresolved, then that is indeed a problem that needs to be resolved!! An effort should be made towards resolution of these unresolved issues as and when they occur. This also gives an opportunity for the analyst to show their abilities. They may need to trace events to more profound causes and constraints and find a quick solution. Continual process improvement techniques are needed to navigate the work and to make the trial a success.

Indicators: Key performance indicators that are chosen for measuring the overall productivity of the system are also useful to highlight the weaknesses of the system and for assessing the effectiveness of alternative course of action. The effectiveness is measured in terms of productivity by measuring speed, accuracy, cost, and flexibility

Requirements traceability matrix

The traceability matrix is based on the relationship between the requirements and the specifications in the requirements documents. Its main function is to implement and validate the software system. The matrix also helps to determine whether the project process is going in the right direction and going accordingly as planned.

Business requirements are mapped by the requirements documents.

The specifications in the requirements documents are mapped by user stories and use cases.

The RTM makes sure that user stories and use cases are traced back to epics which are correlated to each other.

Finally, use cases and use cases are mapped to test cases.

So we know that the requirements traceability matrix, which is a table, shows the relationship between requirements and the specifications in the requirements documents which are ultimately linked to test cases. A *test case* consists of the accurate interlinking of a selected set of documents that make functionality. The matrix is expanded as required so as all functionalities are included. An Excel Spreadsheet can capture traceability. Other tools that can be used are Requisite Pro or Doors and the Sparx enterprise architect. The Sparx enterprise architect provides the users with traceability matrix which can easily link requirements of different levels.

While mapping business requirements to software requirements, a single software requirement can cater to a number of business requirements. The forward traceability is done to track activities from earlier to later in the System Development Life Cycle. Backward traceability is done to trace activities back to business developments.

The RTM links the test cases and requirements and hence it is just a summary and there is no text.

The requirements traceability matrix

Test Cases	Total time	Requirement	Requirement	Requirement

	used	1	2	3
TC1	1	X		
TC2	1			X
TC3	2		X	X
TC4	2	X	X	

Each requirement has a unique requirement id

Requirement 1 is tested by TC 1 and TC4

Requirement 2 is tested by TC3 and TC4

Requirement 3 is tested by TC2 and TC3

The RTM should be created as early as possible in the project and should be kept updated. Workflow changes can cause requirements changes and this in turn again impacts test cases. The matrix is also useful for review purpose before the testing starts.

Software testing and EDP

The main objective of the software concerns the sequencing and utilization of input data to meet the organization's specified requirements. A conglomeration of programs for business operations creates an operational system design that is tested and maintained.

The efficacy of the system is established by testing the system as a whole. Every step in the process analysis deals with either a human task or a business rule or an automated task. The testing is done by operating the software settings in the production environment, *i.e.* in an 'as is - where is' situation. The business processes that have been designed are used within the 'runtime environment' in the 'execution model'. This enables to check whether the software is meeting each and every one of the requirements correctly and whether the software works correctly. Testing enables subsequent debugging, code checking and updating, as the errors are detected in coding and logic. As every module is tested for input layout performance and output accuracy, the system is rated for performance within the existing conditions and options. In this manner, the rapidly tuned business processes modelling provides a solution by working by points and clicks.

Testing requires execution of the software and for this some data has to be entered. Some operations are to be done and then the output is compared to know whether this was the expected data. The testing data is to be identified. *Live test data* may be used, which is the actual data extracted from the files of the organization. *Artificial test data* may be preferred, which are pre –prepared set of data to test various formats and values. The programs are run as a trial with the intention to find errors and to test the logic and control paths and to find out where the program is failing.

If at all there is a problem with any of the features, the requirements document is again scrutinized to identify inadequacies and correct them. In the meanwhile, unnecessary requirements processing will need to be monitored and removed so that the project may be completed on time within the budget.

Test reports

Transactions report on 01/01/2016 of ABC Insurance Ltd.

Name	Policy number	Premium	Receipt Details	Date of renewal	Coinsurance	Reinsurance
A	x	x	x	x	x	x
B	x	x	x	x	x	x
C	x	x	x	x	x	x

Name	Claim Number	Amount	Payment details	Reinstatement
D	x	x	x	x
E	x	x	x	x
F	x	x	x	x

Name	Miscellaneous receipts	Amount	Receipt Details
L	x	x	x
M	x	x	x
N	Y	x	x

Name	Miscellaneous payments	Amount	Payment details
X	x	x	x
Y	x	x	x
Z	x	x	x

Given above is an illustration of a test report. Reports that are tested contain text and/or numbers. Test reports are taken (1) to see designing aspects, (2) whether the additions and other mathematical functions totals, averages and other calculated values are done correctly or not (3) whether the grouping, the sections, the dates and data correlations have been done correctly and (4) whether the data and text is aligned correctly and whether serial numbers, column headers, names, dates and totals are correct and matching with the database. Any discrepancy found between the reports and the database calls for 'debugging' which is done by fixing the source codes. Other factors when testing for performance are (5) performance factors: the time taken compared to the performance requirements for speed and (6) the 'format distributable': which is a specific PDF file for the users which can be opened by an ADOBE reader by the user either from an email attachment or from the website from where they can download it. (7) presentation factors: whether everything is displayed correctly the alignment of data left aligned and right aligned, whether the fonts are uniform or not, whether the presentation style only a read only one where changes cannot be made on it. Regarding the final presentation as a layout or display report, it is established whether the layout as agreed by the user and whether the tables have been drawn correctly. The reports are to be printed clearly and completely and correctly. The presentation and format should be compatible in the printout mode also. Printing of the report test should be correct and clear with the required presentation layout.

Testing strategies

Simulation: Simulation gets the required data about the current quality of the software. The managed business processes, like the underwriting and claims processes, are run as a model before setting them up in a live mode. To enable simulation, data can be categorized as required to generate the required reports. Once the process of simulation is completed, the effectivity and efficiency of the model are established. The defects of the model are found and are reported to the developers. For example: an insurance software should accept specified input data, process data as specified, have different workflows and have specified outputs. The model should have a user interface that has 4 specifications (underwriting premium, claims payments, accounts and investments module and compliance module) and 8 features (RDBMS, automatic backup of data, accessible by PC and mobile, user interface, customer interface, user login, client login, agent login) and 4 performance standards (speed, capacity, security and reliability) which are all stated in the BRD's. In this example, testing the model shows 8 defects in the operational reports. Moreover, it is also found out that the speed is low. What happens next is that the testing data is provided to the other team members, developers, management and the client. Informed decisions are taken after assessing further risks, substantial advantages and improvements. After the analysis of the simulation is made, errors, defects and the potential improvements are identified. The developers fix the errors and defects in the software by identifying the problem in the source code and then fix the problem. After all this has been implemented, then the entire simulation process is done again. As accuracy in the functioning of processes is assigned primary importance, the simulation is made in this accurate manner before finalization. The software can then be shipped to the user within the specified time period.

Code testing: Code testing is done to test the logic of the programs constituting the system. This type of testing examines the logic of the program. An evaluation of the outcome of the tests determine whether the programs need to be corrected; whether they are likely to be correct/ probably correct/ 100% and absolutely correct.

Specification testing: Specification testing is done to state what the program should do and how it performs under various conditions. Specifications refer to how the program should respond when inputs or combinations of inputs are used for enabling functionality.

Product testing: Product testing verifies whether the ongoing development processes are according to the specified requirements. This type of testing shows how the system is accessed by the users, what data is processed and how the reports are designed. Ultimately, the system is to be availed by the customer at the upfront and monitored by the user at the backend and hence, should be user friendly.

Unit and Systems Testing: The popular preference is that both individual and systems testing should be done. *Unit testing* is for each module separately. Test cases exercise each and every scenario. Interactions between modules are done by *systems testing* to estimate its capacity and accuracy. It answers questions about whether the system can handle activities at peak load and store transaction data either on a disk or in other files. Other queries answered by system testing is about the time taken to process a transaction and whether the system can recover lost data and can be restarted after a failure, whether the actual working is accurate as specified in the user manual, and how the system is to be used to process data and prepare reports.

Acceptance Testing: The user takes the entire system and tests it to confirm whether it is according to their requirements.

Conversion

The process of conversion involves changing from the old system to the new one. There are four methods of conversion:

Parallel approach: This refers to the situation when both the old and the new systems are made to run together. The old system will provide a fall back in the event that the new system should fail at any point in time.

Direct approach: In this approach, the new system is introduced abruptly sometimes over a weekend or overnight. This type of direct conversion requires careful planning ahead of implementation as the old system has been discontinued and cannot be a fall back.

Pilot approach: The new system is installed on an experimental basis before it is finally implemented.

Phased in approach: The new system is installed step –by-step and carefully, in phases.

Problem tracking

All through the formation of the system, there should be a clear correlation between the requirements and the corresponding valuation. Hence, the proposed solution is solicited by monitoring the product backlog and the release note. If a problem does arise, its impact towards the whole solution should be determined. Keeping organizational goals in viewpoint, the solution could be traced to a much nobler cause. The timely resolution of issues in an effective way is necessary to complete the project. The questions that need to be tackled are:

A process has been made or altered. Do they touch all the elements? Do they cause a positive effect? Have some substantial changes been enabled? Has the business process system been able to merge with the existing applications and systems? As the effort and initiative have been costly and/or risky, has improvement been inculcated as part of the process? Have the considerations of the estimated payback time and the profitability turnover been met with.

Integration

All the processes that are interlinked enable the system as to work as a whole. This is also known as called integration. A special document called 'user manual' is prepared to help with issues in integration. The user manual traces functions within the system that helps the user to navigate within the system. With the help of the user manual, the persons who have been adequately trained to use the well designed and technically elegant system are able to login and work with the system. The components of a user manual are given below:

USER MANUAL	
#Sequence of operations	#Start –up –

	procedures
#Possible error messages, explanations	# Menu tree
#Back – up – procedure	# Recovery procedures

Documentation

Product designs of the system are represented by input and output layouts in the computer interface. *Documentation for the insurance system* begins with defining the functional and non – functional business requirements documents (BRD's). *User documentations* are built according to the work and the work –flow between different departments. User documents are defined when product requirements are specified and includes issuance of proposal, underwriting layouts and reports, claims processing layouts and reports, accounting layouts and reports, customer servicing and other management reports.

Document management and maintenance enables business information to be accurately represented. Documents are made easily available for work and for upgrading the process redesign. Proper enterprise documentation is also vital for adhering to compliance and vigilance and for audit support and screening.

Some strategies when things are behind schedule

Possible causes for failure of projects include the following reasons: Maybe the project chosen was incorrect. The processes may not have been correct. There may have been a lack of coordination and cooperation between the participants and/or partners. There may have been some technology inadequacy. Process analysis can help discover more efficient and logical ways of doing things. Consider redesigning the stories as being smaller. This makes things more manageable as larger stories are difficult to estimate and complete wholly. Consider accurate information about the domain and also clear and stable BRD's. Add charts and diagrams which are easier to interpret when compared with words. Documentation should be well done and if necessary can be broken down further to make thing less complicated. Assess the skill sets, education and strengths' of individuals in the team and solicit further collaboration for getting more access to the required software and for help when needed. Keep a tab on the key questions and processes of the development life cycle.

Systems auditing

The service components of business include end to end business processes, human tasks and business rules which have been architected for reuse for a more flexible business processes. System auditing is made to evaluate whether a system is doing what it was supposed to do.

A new, upgraded or an altered system may at any times become necessary due to changes in the organizational structure or government policies. Sometimes technological changes and innovations in the hardware and software environment cause the need for maintaining and upgrading system. Systems review and identification of unsatisfactory features and suggests amendments are all part of systems auditing. Systems auditing keeps track of the performance of programs, the throughput, the output effectivity, documentation, constraints, the operational and interface difficulties and recommends further action if required.

The common software platform should be simple to work with; while at the same time should be robust. It should allow for process improvement and also innovation of business process. As customer rating of the company improves, their loyalty index will also improve which is what is needed to meet the challenging market situations.

There is an important consideration here. Technology, in its very nature involves innovation as time passes on. The next step in innovation has brought forward emerging roles in cloud computing and big data analytics. And so, we can certainly expect the path of innovation to keep taking us into new domains in the area of technology, all of which will require system auditing.

Exercises

What is the importance of the traceability matrix?

What are the various testing strategies?

The first sign of automation when a Frenchman named **Joseph Marie Jaquard**, during 1801, invented tabulating machines to operate his cloth weaving machine. Automation was furthered when punch cards for data processing were developed in 1880 by **Dr Herman Hollerith.** The next major stage of innovation was when **Charles Babbage** had built the difference engine in 1822, which was specially designed to compute polynomials. The first real concept of artificial intelligence was born in 1936, when a 24 year old mathematician named **Alan Tuning** from Cambridge University worked on Charles Babbage's invention. He established that a machine can be made 'intelligent'. Subsequently, machines were designed to compute, store and process data and since then generations of computers have been evolving.

Innovations:

Automation for information management has been the inevitable outcome of innovations. The earliest applications of innovations in information management in the modern office were Microsoft office word, excel, power point, one –note, outlook and desk–top publishing (Page maker and Photoshop) which enables publishing of books with pictures.

Modern IT has evolved from electronic data processing (EDP) of the recent past. Here, data is directly entered into programmed electronic devices.

Then the data is analyzed by programs within the electronic device, to serve some purpose. Data is stored in various storage devices including floppy disks, magnetic tapes, hard disk, and cloud servers.

With modern industry EDP applications came the automation of real time business transactions, cross-selling, tracking of customers visit to website, contacting customers via website contact form or by e-mail, tracking of customers' preferences by analytics, customer care services and ATM facilities.

Computer languages

A major advance in the world of innovations has been made by 'computer languages' in automation. Computer languages communicate by employing 'signals' which enables an on and off function by using the binary digits 0 and 1. These form a means of 'communication' and provide an interface between the user and the computer.

Computer languages have advanced over the years. Higher level languages (HLL) enable grouping of data and the use of English. HLL create 'programmes' which are interpreted by the computers 'translators and interpreters'.

Computer languages:

First generation languages: Initially, low level languages were written using binary digits 0 and 1. These were popularly known as machine language or assembly language. The computer responds to this language via electrical signals and does not need compilers and interpreters to respond.

Middle level languages: Middle level languages enabled the ease of grouping and processing of data while working with binary digits. They included C and BASIC. They offered the flexibility of low level languages and also enabled flow charting. Data grouping and processing and flow charting enabled the basics of programming. This also led to the formation of high level languages.

High level languages: These were the third generation of languages. The significant feature here was the use of English words for programs that gave instructions to the computer. Some examples of HLL include BASIC, FORTRAN, PASCAL, COBOL and C:

Fourth level languages: Fourth level languages have added user friendliness. They come as 'software packages'. They have arithmetic functionalities and report generation capabilities. They also have database management capabilities, graphical user interface and web development capabilities. Some examples include PHP, Ruby for versatility. FOCUS,

SQL, Oracle, Ingress and Sybase, Quest for data base, data analysis and reports. Visual data flex and MATLAB for creating GUI.

Interpreters, assemblers, compilers and linkers: These are crucial as they compose special programs which enable HLL, with which programing is done, to be translated into low level machine code instructions which the computer can understand.

Utility programs: These are small programs supplied by the manufacturers. They enable routine housekeeping functions including making backups, copying files, clean disk, disk fragmentation and the like. Additional utilities from third parties may also be installed.

The constituents of computer software

'Software is used to control the computer and develop and run applications. It includes programs such as operating systems, database managers, compilers, Web servers, router operating systems and control programs for other network devices': The PC Magazine Encyclopedia.

Operating system: These are the standard programs developed for the computer. These control the operations of the computer. They are primarily provided along with the computer system by the manufacturer. They are formed as a set of programs and are primarily installed to control the input, storage and output functions correlating the hardware device and software utilities. They also provide an interface for communication between the user and the computer as a device/machine. They have help menus and provide error messages and contain commands to use and navigate within the system. Some popular operating systems are MSDOS, UNIX, WINDOWS, LINUX MACINTOSH, ANDROID and iPad.

Database: The database managers are programs which enable the storage of large amount of data. Data is arranged and extracted in different formats to enable meaningful information to be obtained and printed. Some popular database packages, also known as RDBMS, include Sybase, Ingress, and Informix and Microsoft SQL server.

Application Software: These are a specialized set of computer programs. They work with the operating system. Application software enables specific data processing tasks. In other words, application programs are made to complete user tasks such as creating related documentation, creating database, accessing the internet and even playing games!! Some off the shelf application software include Microsoft office, Adobe creative suite and Sony audio master and the web browser.

System software: The operating system, the database and the application software together constitute the system software. These programs make the computer obey and respond to a certain set of instructions that are given in a logical manner.

Application software for Insurance was initially developed by IBM. They were followed by other major players in the market who developed various constituents and processes. Business programming were done with HLL programming languages like objective - oriented COBOL, JAVA, C#, SWIFT and RUST. The core application software modules in an insurance company include:

Core Insurance Operations: Underwriting and policy servicing, claims, accounts and management services.

Risk, Finance and Corporate Governance: Investment planning, funds flow and cash flow planning, risk management, corporate governance and compliance.

CRM: Sales, marketing and marketing analytics, customer relationship management solutions.

HRM: Human resource management, payroll, income tax statements, employee leave records, department and place of employment and employee benefits.

Exercise:

Outline the functions of computer languages and their applications.

Hint: Identify the first generation computer languages and their functions and then study the advancements since then.

Annexure 1: Context diagram of an insurance system

Annexure 2: Representation of a simplified underwriting and policy management system.

Annexure 3: Representation of a simplified insurance accounting system

Annexure 4: Representation of a simplified investment system

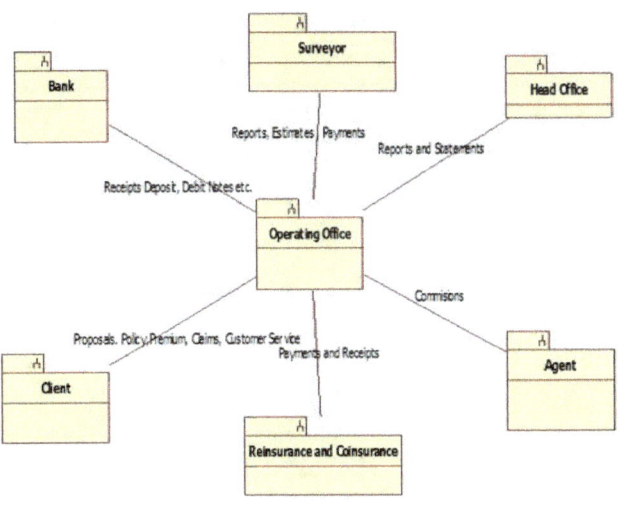

Representation of a Simplified Underwriting and Policy Management System

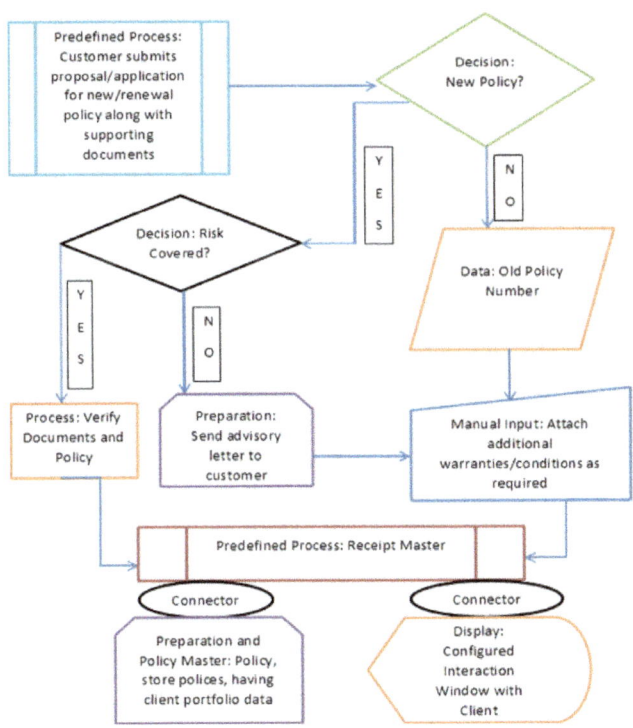

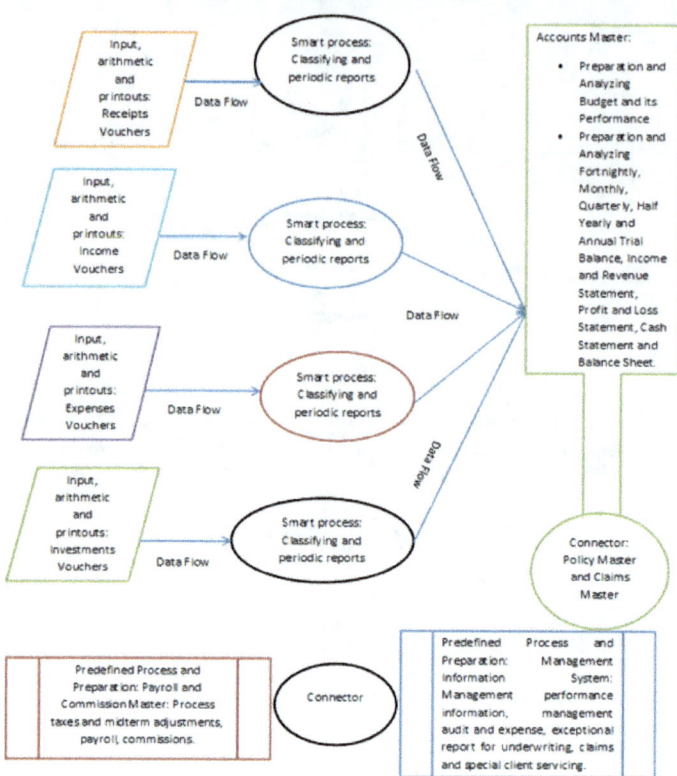

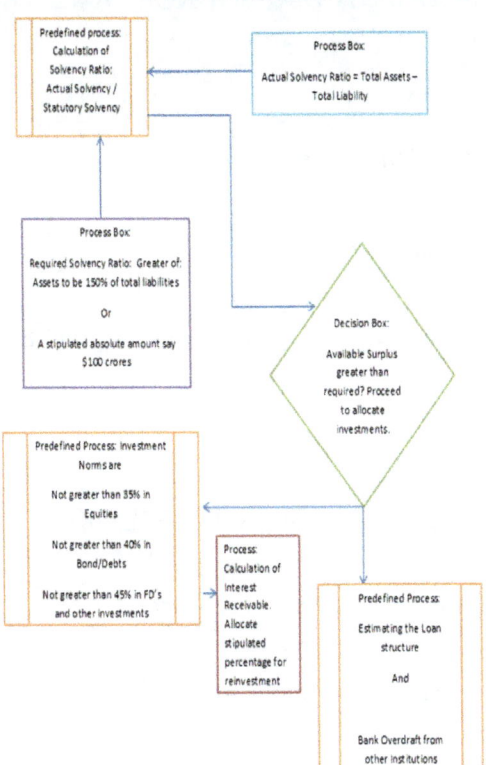

1) *Certification in business analysis*

2) *Programming tools:*

https://sourceforge.net/projects/staruml/?source=directory

And

https://www.visual-paradigm.com/download/

3) *Open source insurance software.*

https://sourceforge.net/projects/oquote/?source=directory

ABOUT THE AUTHOR

Kavita Sinha comes from a background of professional Finance and Insurance. She has completed her under – graduation in Economics from Delhi University and graduated in Economics from the University of Madras, served for a public – sector insurance company for seventeen years before becoming an author. She holds a PGDM (Fin and CRM) from Symbiosis International University and is a Fellow of the Insurance Institute of India.